MO

Tibetan Divination System

MO

Tibetan Divination System

The examination of what should be accepted and what should be discarded of the good and bad through relying upon the king of mantras, AH RA PA TSA, which is known as the speech of the Pleasing Manjushri.

by Mipham

Foreword by His Holiness Sakya Trizin
Translated into English by Jay Goldberg and
Lobsang Dakpa
Accompanying card deck designed and illustrated by
Doya Nardin

Snow Lion Publications
Ithaca, New York USA

Snow Lion Publications
P.O. Box 6483
Ithaca, NY 14851
USA

Printed in the USA

ISBN 0-937938-74-2

Contents

Foreword

The ever-increasing wealth of books concerned with Tibetan culture and religion has both influenced and broadened the outlook of the West. A few of these publications have dealt with our life and culture in a balanced way, discussing them in their proper context. However, the majority of books have looked at one aspect of Tibet, in isolation from the whole. This may leave the reader with a disjointed view of Tibet.

The work presented here—*MO: Tibetan Divination System*—should be seen against the entire backdrop of Tibetan culture. The Mo should not be seen as a spurious religious practice, unconnected with the profound teachings of the Buddha which underlie the life of the Tibetan people.

In Buddhism, especially in the Mahayana tradition, it has been taught that the highest good is to benefit other living beings. This is exemplified by the bodhisattva, a being who strives to gain the stage of pure and perfect enlightenment for the sake of all sentient beings. Numerous scriptures tell us that a bodhisattva should not hesitate to use any method that would bring relative and ultimate happiness to others. The bodhisattva has been enjoined to assist others by giving them spiritual teachings, material objects such as medicine and food, fearlessness, loving kindness and advice on how to deal with the travails of worldly existence.

Since the Buddhas are endowed with knowledge of the cause and effect of all conditions as well as insight into their ultimate reality, the use of Mo could prove beneficial if combined with unwavering faith in and one-pointed concentration upon the Buddhas. Mo is thus one of the ways in which unenlightened beings may rely upon the Buddhas to help overcome predicaments in their everyday lives.

There are two primary functions of the Mo. First of all, it is a system that allows us to help ourselves to see a situation or event clearly. Secondly, if we use it for others with the proper motivation of performing a selfless act of giving—as has been extensively done by many of the great teachers of Tibet—it is a system that enhances our practice of the Bodhisattva's path. There is also a secondary function of the Mo. The central, most profound teaching of the Buddha is *Pratitya Samutpada*, which may be translated as interdependent origination or co-dependent arising. This teaching simultaneously explains the essence of the interplay of causes and conditions on the relative, worldly level of reality and the essence of emptiness or selflessness on the ultimate level of reality. Although diligent efforts are needed in concentration and insight to attain a realization of interdependent origination, a system such as Mo reveals a glimpse of the interdependence and causal play of the world in which we live and may hopefully induce one to investigate it on a deeper level.

Many methodologies of Mo have been utilized in Tibet. The system here, compiled by the great master Jamgon Mipham from the sacred Tantras expounded by the Buddha, obtains its authority from the spiritual power and wisdom of Manjushri—the Bodhisattva who embodies the transcendental knowledge of all the Buddhas. It is Manjushri's speech as epitomized in his holy mantra, OM AH RA PA TSA NA DHIH, and the sanctity of his all-pervasive wisdom that empower one to obtain an accurate answer that reflects the interplay of conditions concerning the situation and it's outcome. In the *Manjushri Nama Samgiti* (Chanting the Names of Manjushri), the Buddha himself extolled the great qualities of Manjushri and stated that the mantra of Manjushri, OM AH RA PA TSA NA DHIH, is an expression of the wisdom experienced by all enlightened beings. Therefore, by relying upon the compassionate blessings of Manjushri and the power of his mantra, you should have no doubt that the wisdom of all enlightened beings is manifesting itself in the throw of the dice.

The two translators of *MO: Tibetan Divination System*, Lobsang Dagpa and Jay Goldberg, have explored the Dharma at many levels and their understanding of the scriptures is clearly seen in the fine work they have produced here. This translation together with the beautiful paintings created for the text, presents to the English-speaking world another addition to the accurate and growing body of literature concerning our land of Tibet.

H.H. Sakya Trizin

Introduction

In Tibet, the use of the Mo, or predictive technique, has been heavily relied upon throughout the centuries, as it has been the general practice of Tibetans to consult some method of prognostication when questions arise concerning various occurrences in their lives—bad dreams, the arising of an illness, the undertaking of some work or travel, or even the wish to engage in spiritual disciplines or practices.

A great variety of methods have been used to extract omens for the future. The use of dice, as presented in this book, is only one of those methods, one coming down to us from ancient times. The various predictive techniques which employ the use of dice are related to different deities within the tantric tradition—generally, the Protectors of the Dharma are the type of deity most relied upon. In this specific case, however, it is the great Bodhisattva of Wisdom, Manjushri, whose blessings and advice are sought in order to ascertain an answer for one's problems or inquiry. Since Manjushri is recognized as the embodiment of the wisdom of all the Buddhas of the past, present and future, people have been confident over the centuries that he would properly guide them through the vicissitudes of worldly existence and lead them through his transcendent wisdom to accept what was most beneficial and to abandon all that would be of harm. Furthermore, they trusted that his guidance would eventually lead them to the state of ultimate peace and enlightenment.

Based primarily upon the *Kalacakra Tantra* and with supplementary explanations from *The Ocean of Dakinis* and other texts, this prediction manual of the mantra AH RA PA TSA NA DHI was composed by Jamgon Mipham (Jamyang Namgyal Gyatso), 1846-1912, a great saint and scholar of the Nyingmapa tradition. Jamgon Mipham is considered one of the great luminaries of Tibet during this past century, due primarily to his scholarship and continual practice of the Buddha's teaching. Born in eastern Tibet, his principal teachers were Jamyang Khyentse Wangpo and Patrul Rinpoche. With them and others, he studied the doctrines of the four main schools of Tibetan Buddhism as well as the five major and five minor subjects of scholarship, such as poetry, astrology, medicine, grammar, logic and philosophy. He was renowned for his lucid explanations of the Sutras and Tantras found within the teachings of the Buddha, though within the more than thirty-two volumes of his writings are found works concerning the architectural methods for constructing temples and houses, astrology, methods of casting predictions (with an entire volume dedicated to the explanation of a Bonpo method for revealing future events through the tying of various knots), poetry, and a vast array of other subjects. In brief, he was a consummate scholar as well as a great practitioner of the path of Dharma.

THE METHOD FOR USING THIS DIVINATION MANUAL

Before making a divination, it is recommended that you perform a few preliminary meditations. First of all, imagine that the great Bodhisattva of Wisdom, Manjushri, is in the sky in front of you. His body is yellow, with one face and two hands. His right hand holds aloft the flaming sword of wisdom, while his left hand holds at his heart the stem of a blue lotus flower. The flower blossoms beside his left ear, and upon it rests a copy of *The Book of the Perfection of Wisdom (Prajnaparamita)*. His two feet are crossed in the vajra posture and he appears in the form of a sixteen-year-old boy. Thinking that he is blessing the dice with which you are going to make the prediction, recite the following verse:

> Om, the magnificent Manjushri who possesses the eye of transcendental wisdom which unobstructedly sees all three times,[1] please take heed of me. Through the power of the truth of the non-deceiving, interdependently arising Three Jewels[2] and Three Roots,[3] please make clear what should be accepted and what discarded.

Next, you should recite the mantra of Manjushri:

OM AH RA PA TSA NA DHI,[4]

and the mantra of Interdependent Origination:

OM YEDHARMA HETU PRABHAWA HETUNTE KHEN TATHAGATO HAYA WATET TE KHEN TSAYO NIRODHA EWAM WADI MAHA SHRAMANA SOHA.[5]

---

[1]Three times refers to the past, present and future.

[2]Three Jewels refers to the Buddha, his teaching (Dharma) and his followers (Sangha).

[3]Three Roots refers to the Guru, one's special meditation deity (Yidam) and the feminine energies (Dakinis).

[4]This mantra, which is pronounced OM AH RA PA CHA NA DEE, is one of the principal mantras of Manjushri. Though having no specific translation, the five middle syllables—AH RA PA TSA NA—are said to represent the five families of the Buddhas, while the final syllable, DHI, represents the wisdom of all the Buddhas.

[5]This mantra, which is pronounced OM/ YEA DAR MA/ HEH TOO/ PRA BAH WAH/ HEH TUN TAY/ KEN/ TA T'A GA TOE/ HA YA/ WA TET/ TAY/ KEN/ CHA YO/ NEE RO DA/ EH WAM/ WA DEE/ MA HA/ SHRA MA NA/ SO HA, may be roughly translated as: The Tathagata (Buddha) has explained the origin of those things which arise from a cause; their cessation too he has explained; this is the doctrine

The first mantra should be recited three or seven times (or more, if you wish), and the second mantra should be recited one, three or seven times. In conclusion, blow upon the dice to endow it with the power of the mantras. Then, keeping in mind your question and also the name of the person for whom you are casting the prediction (if it is not being thrown on your own behalf), cast the dice two times and then examine the answer. For example, if after the first throw of the dice the letter RA appears, and after the second the letter DHI appears, then you should search for the answer RA DHI which is number 12.

THE ANSWERS

Each answer of this prediction system is divided into several parts. First, the name of the answer is given; the lead paragraph explains the name using metaphors and symbols, while the next paragraph characterizes the answer often by quoting some source in order to show the general trend of the answer. Following this, eleven categories are listed with specific predictions for each, and finally a supplementary name is given.

The eleven main categories cover all the possible questions that you put forth to the book. They are listed below, with a brief description of the realm of experience that each covers.

Family/property and life: foundations of your life, including anything dealing with your physical life or vitality, your family and property.

Intentions and aims: the goals and aims you may seek within your business, as well as other aspects of your life.

Friends and wealth: the people you associate with as well as your financial affairs and business affairs.

Enemies: description of any enemies you may have.

---

of the great sage. This mantra is actually a pith instruction of the Buddha's profound insight into interdependent origination.

Guests: this category was necessary in Tibet where it might take a guest several months to arrive, so there was always a concern for visitors en route.

Illness: the state of your health.

Evil spirits: possibility of your troubles arising from some negative forces, such as spirits or unwholesome environmental conditions.

Spiritual practice: obstacles and outlook for spiritual practices.

Lost article: whether a lost article can be found and where.

Will they come, and will the task be accomplished: the meeting with another and the possibility of accomplishing some work.

All remaining matters: covers any other question which may not fall under any of the above categories.

Not only are answers given, but also advice is proffered regarding how to overcome particular problems. Generally, a specific spiritual practice, a ritual or the reliance upon a certain deity is proposed. The common Tibetan did not have the ability to perform these rituals or meditations, so it was (and continues to be) the practice for the querent to approach the local monastery or those who were learned in the performance of rituals to do whatever was needed on his or her behalf. Therefore, although you may be unfamiliar with some of the names of deities, rituals and texts, the authors left them in the translation with the thought that you may have the opportunity to approach someone with that knowledge. Once these remedies are understood they can be used by the inquirer to help overcome the problem or to accomplish one's aims and wishes.

To ascertain whether an answer is very firm or weak, it is

advisable to throw the dice two more times. If the same two syllables are repeated, then this means that your answer is very firm. If the two syllables reverse themselves, then the answer is a weak one. If the two syllables of the subsequent toss are different, then your answer is good as it stands.

You can also look into the answer from other perspectives. For example, whether the prediction is favorable or unfavorable for the present time, it is good to perform another throw of the dice in regards to the future. In this way you can make predictions for different times. If the question you ask is a very serious one, such as one concerning a major illness, then it is good to make several predictions about it. If it is only a small matter, then one prediction is enough.

SUPPLEMENTARY INTERPRETIVE MATERIAL

The six syllables of the dice allow for a range of interpretation. Several levels of meaning are listed below.

In a sense, there is an outer and inner meaning to the syllables and their relationship to each other. It is said that if the two syllables appear the same, such as DHI DHI, PA PA, etc., then the outer and inner meanings are the same.

In regards to your relations with others, you can throw two predictions. The first concerns yourself, while the second concerns the other person. Otherwise, even within one prediction you can regard the first syllable to represent yourself while the second syllable represents the other person. Then examine the relationship between the two syllables.

When the syllable DHI appears first, we can see the following meanings:

if DHI DHI appears, this indicates increasing;

if DHI AH appears, this indicates equanimity;

if DHI RA appears, this indicates unimpeded continuity;

if DHI TSA appears, this indicates favorableness and the likelihood of the quick accomplishment of the question;

if DHI PA appears, this indicates that activities such as marriage, engagements, and the like will be good.

If the syllable DHI appears as the second part of the answer, then this is not bad and the propitiation of deities will find success. The appearance of the syllable DHI portents increasing for those who had nothing previously.

If the syllable AH appears first in the combination, then the answer is only mediocre. If it appears as the second part of the answer, then you will have no obstacles in regards to your inquiry. In regards to curing a disease, the appearance of the syllable AH is good.

The syllable RA is concerned with the desires of your mind; the syllable TSA is concerned with messages; PA with the joy of your property; while NA is connected with your area or country.

The syllables AH, DHI, RA and TSA have insight wisdom, violence and the waning moon in common, while NA and PA have concentration, gentleness and the waxing moon in common. Furthermore, RA represents the voice and speech, TSA the airs of the body (this also includes the breath and so is in relation to air diseases), while NA represents the body and PA the veins of the body.

In regards to various types of activities:

PA is for activities of peace or purification;
RA is for activities of power or subduing;
NA is for activities of increasing or prosperity;
TSA is for activities of violence or destruction;
DHI is for activities of excellence; while
AH pervades all activities.

In regards to the elements:

AH represents empty space;

RA represents fire;
PA represents water;
TSA represents air;
NA represents earth; while
DHI represents transcendental wisdom.

In regards to the parts of the body:

RA represents the eye;
AH represents the ear;
NA represents the nose;
PA represents the tongue;
TSA represents the body; while
DHI represents the mind.

In regards to the objects of the senses:

RA represents forms;
AH represents sounds;
NA represents odors;
PA represents tastes;
TSA represents tactile objects; while
DHI represents thoughts.

In regards to the inner parts of the body:

RA represents the heart and small intestines;
AH represents the lungs and large intestines;
NA represents the gall bladder and stomach;
PA represents the kidneys, the organ which holds
  urine, and the reproductive organs;
TSA represents the liver; while
DHI represents the semen.

In regards to the spheres of the world:

AH and DHI represent the sky;
NA and PA represent the earth; while
RA and TSA represent the area between the earth and
  sky.

In regards to gender:

NA and PA are female;
DA and TSA are male; while
AH and DHI are neuter or hermaphrodite.

In regards to directions which will indicate the direction a thief or someone else has gone, where a lost article may be found, the direction in which one should move, and the like:

AH and DHI are central;
PA is south;
RA is west;
TSA is north;
NA is east; while
AH may also be said to pervade all the directions so it indicates no specific direction of its own.

In regards to color:

RA is red;
PA is white;
TSA is green;
NA is yellow;
DHI is multi-colored; while
AH is neutral with no specific color of its own.

In regards to shapes:

RA is a triangle;
PA is a circle;
TSA is a semi-circle;
NA is a square;
DHI is various shapes; while
AH has no specific shape of its own.

In regards to the Buddha families:

AH is the Tathagata Race of Vairocana;
RA is the Lotus Race of Amitabha;
PA is the Jewel Race of Ratnasambhava;

TSA is the Karma Race of Amoghasiddhi; NA is the Vajra Race of Akshobhya; while DHI is the Heruka Race of Vajradhara.

KEY TO THE DIVINATIONS

1. AH AH, The Stainless Sky
2. AH RA, The Flaming Rays of the Sun
3. AH PA, The Nectar Rays of the Moon
4. AH TSA, The Bright Star
5. AH NA, The Ground of Gold
6. AH DHI, The Tone of Vajras
7. RA AH, The Bright Lamp
8. RA RA, Adding Butter to the Burning Flames
9. RA PA, The Demon of Death
10. RA TSA, The King of Power
11. RA NA, The Dried-up Tree
12. RA DHI, The Door of Auspicious Visions
13. PA AH, The Vase of Nectar
14. PA RA, The Pool Without a Source of Water
15. PA PA, The Ocean of Nectar
16. PA TSA, The Demon of Afflictions
17. PA NA, The Golden Lotus
18. PA DHI, The Nectar-like Medicine
19. TSA AH, The White Umbrella of Good Fortune
20. TSA RA, The Great Fiery Weapon
21. TSA PA, Empty of Intelligence
22. TSA TSA, The Streamer of Fame
23. TSA NA, The Mara Demon of the Aggregates
24. TSA DHI, The House of Good Tidings
25. NA AH, The Golden Mountain
26. NA RA, The Demon of the Heavenly Son
27. NA PA, The Overflowing Jeweled Vessel
28. NA TSA, The Scattered Mountain of Sand
29. NA NA, The Mansion of Gold
30. NA DHI, The Treasury of Jewels
31. DHI AH, Manjushri Appears
32. DHI RA, The Endless, Auspicious Knot
33. DHI PA, The Golden Female Fish
34. DHI TSA, The White Conch
35. DHI NA, The Golden Wheel
36. DHI DHI, The Jeweled Banner of Victory

Manjushri   Painting by Doya Nardin.

THE DIVINATION MANUAL

1. AH AH, The Stainless Sky

If AH AH—the stainless sky—appears, then the inquirer should listen. Just as the sky is free from stains, so your mind should be completely purified and placed in equanimity.

The sign of this divination is "the sound of threefold emptiness."

Family/property and life: There is no harm to your family, property and life, and they will be very happy.

Intentions and aims: Since there is equanimity, there will be no obstructions to the fulfillment of your intentions and aims. This AH AH prediction is the most propitious for averting negative forces and bad omens. If you rely upon the Buddhas and Bodhisattvas, then obscurations will be cleared and results will be quickly obtained. If you had previous troubles or unhappiness, these will be righted.

Friends and wealth: Though you have friends and wealth, it will be difficult for them to remain with you in the future. If you desire to retain them, you should make offerings of flowers and the like to the *Prajnaparamita Sutras*—the discourses on the Perfection of Wisdom.

Enemies: There are no enemies.

Guests: There will be a smooth and comfortable journey for the guests that you are expecting.

Illness and evil spirits: It is seen that you are healthy, and there are no negative forces or evil spirits whatsoever bothering you.

Spiritual practice: There will be success in abandoning unwholesome tendencies and in accomplishing meditation. Faults and obscurations will be completely purified.

Lost article: If it is still near the location where you left it, it will be found. Otherwise, it will be difficult to regain.

Will they come, and will the task be accomplished: There are equal chances either way. So things can be accomplished, but only slowly.

All remaining matters: There is also only an average chance of success in regards to any other inquiry. In order to make the questioned matter possible and to make it successful, you should rely upon Vajrasattva as your special deity, recite the One Hundred Syllable Mantra of Vajrasattva, and recite any of the long, middle or short *Prajnaparamita Sutras*. Also, you can rely upon Akashagarbha as a special deity.

This prediction is known as "the giving of fearlessness."

2. *AH RA,*
The Flaming Rays of the Sun

If AH RA—the flaming rays of the sun—appears, then whatever the inquirer asks will be unreservedly settled like the clarity of the sun, and it will be very good.

The sign of this divination is known as "dustless and clear."

Family/property and life: Your family, property and life will be good if you diligently engage in virtuous deeds.

Intentions and aims: If you cut the net of doubt enveloping yourself, then they will turn out well.

Friends and wealth: If you obtain shiny articles such as crystals, gems and the like, or red colored articles, then there will be a slight improvement.

Enemies: There are no enemies.

Guests: Your guests will journey with ease, and you will hear precise, pleasing news concerning them.

Illness and evil spirits: You will quickly recover from your illness, and there is no trouble from evil spirits.

Spiritual practice: Through practice your intelligence, learning and contemplation will increase.

Lost article: If you search in a southwesterly direction from where it has been lost, then it will be found. Someone will come to give you news about it.

Will they come, and will the task be accomplished: The meaning of this will be clearly known to you.

All remaining matters: Although the prediction for all remaining questions are quite all right, nevertheless the outcome of work involving earth, houses, and objects which are used as supports—such as tables and so on—is slightly bad. If you rely upon wisdom deities such as Manjushri, offer butter lamps and prayer flags, and recite various sutras such as *Dispelling the Darkness in the Ten Directions*, then the work will turn out well.

This prediction is known as "the departing of darkness."

3. *AH PA, Nectar Rays of the Moon*

If AH PA—the good moon—appears, then just as the rays of nectar, the moon, illumine the sky, so the accomplishment of peaceful, increasing and virtuous activities is assured.

The sign of this divination is called "the enjoyment of sense-desire objects where there is no assemblage of obstacles."

Family/property and life: If you perform the rituals of cleansing pollutions and of washing, then you will be able to increase the number of your children.

Intentions and aims: There are no obstacles in regards to your intentions and aims. It is especially good to perform gentle, peaceful activities; a strong effect will not arise through power or violent activities.

Friends and wealth: All white colored objects, food and drink will increase.

Enemies: There are no enemies.

Guests: Your guests' journeys will be comfortable, and they will arrive soon.

Illness: You will quickly recover from cold and indigestive diseases.

Evil spirits: There are no evil spirits bothering you whatsoever.

Spiritual practice: The virtuous mind is good and virtues will increase.

Lost article: If you request a woman to investigate in a southern or northern direction, then the object will be found.

Will they come, and will the task be accomplished: It will be accomplished.

All remaining matters: It is predicted that works involving women and any easy, non-strenuous activities are good. Any activity involving fire is slightly bad. Little things and happiness will increase by relying upon female deities such as White Tara and Ushnisha Vijaya. You should recite any sutra in which predictions for enlightenment are given to women. Perform the water giving ritual and water washing ritual to avoid punishment. It is very good if you perform offerings to nagas. Also, through relying upon any guru-yoga practice, good results will arise.

This prediction is known as "dense, good clouds."

4. AH TSA, The Bright Star

If AH TSA—the very bright star—appears, then, if you work with steadfastness and carefulness of mind, there will be a good result.

The sign of this divination is known as "the non-dispersion of the beautiful accumulation which has been gathered."

Family/property and life: If you hang prayer flags and burn incense then all of these will turn out well.

Intentions and aims: Any activity which involves going, traveling and movement, as well as acts of giving, will have good results.

Friends and wealth: You will receive wooden articles, animals, green cloth and the like, in addition to news and letters.

Enemies: There are no enemies.

Guests: Your guests will have comfortable journeys and will arrive very, very soon.

Illness: An air illness and agitation of the mind are present, but they are not very bad. It would be helpful if you were to worship your ancestors, make offerings to tree spirits, and the like.

Evil spirits: Though there are no evil spirits attacking you, there is the slight fault of having too many agitated, fickle thoughts. Through relying upon steadiness and firmness of mind, things will turn out well.

Spiritual practice: Any type of spiritual practice will have a good result, especially if you do it in a location other than where you usually practice.

Lost article: Although it has been taken by another person, it is possible to find it should you search quickly in a northern or eastern direction from where it was lost.

Will they come, and will the task be accomplished: It is said that it will be accomplished.

All remaining matters: These will be positive, although any activity involving water is slightly unfavorable. You should rely upon activity deities such as Green Tara. Perform ritual offerings to the Dharma Protectors, and hang as many prayer flags as possible. Perform circumambulations, prostrations and torma-throwing rituals. Recite any sutras, such as the *Buddha Avatamsaka Sutra* and those involving stories of the Buddhas and Bodhisattvas going to other lands. If green deities are relied upon, all activities will be quickly accomplished.

Thus this prediction is known as "increasing the power of air like the revolution of the energy currents in the sky."

5. AH NA, *The Ground of Gold*

If AH NA—the ground of gold—appears, then steady work will be accomplished and have good results, just as the earth is good.

The sign of this divination is known as "the inability to guess accurately so that the answer will remain unresolved."

Family/property and life: Family, property and life are very stable and are in excellent condition.

Intentions and aims: Since your intention is firm, it is advisable to remain in your own location. Then your plan will not be aborted.

Friends and wealth: The long-term future is good, but it will take some time to obtain it.

Enemies: There are no enemies.

Guests: Generally their journey is good, but it will be some time before they arrive.

Illness: There is a slight phlegm disease, but it is not bad. It will be difficult to cure the disease immediately, so you should perform a fire ritual, erect "mani" prayer wheels that are turned by the wind, and hang many prayer flags.

Evil spirits: There are no evil spirits bothering you. The blame for your trouble should be placed upon the unsuitableness of the earth and water in your locale.

Spiritual practice: The future is good, and this is especially true should you practice continually in one place.

Lost article: It will be found by one of your own people. Otherwise, search in an eastern direction from where it was lost. If it isn't found quickly, then it will be difficult to find in the future.

Will they come, and will the task be accomplished: It will take some time, so don't be overly enthusiastic.

All remaining matters: If done quickly, things will turn out well. However, any activity involving air, the sending of letters, news and the like, is unfavorable. It is good if you rely upon Vajra deities such as Shakyamuni, Acala, and so on, as well as on Quality or Jewel deities like Ratnasambhava. Also, it is good to perform wealth-propitiating rituals, make a hundred thousand small earth stupas, carve mantras upon rocks, erect images, and make offerings to earth gods.

This prediction is known as "if you stay here, the basis will become firm."

6. *AH DHI, The Tone of the Vajra*

If AH DHI, Vajra Saraswati—the tone of the vajra—appears, then the happiness of mind will increase as it does when one hears good news, and all will be good.

The sign of this divination is known as "increasing the measure-less intelligence by the goddess of mind." Generally speaking, this divination augurs well for the studies of science, arts and Buddhist scriptures.

Family/property and life: If you perform long-life meditations and rituals of female deities, then your life will be firm and stable.

Intentions and aims: You will achieve them.

Friends and wealth: There is quite a good chance of happiness.

Enemies: Enemies will not arise, and the gods will protect you.

Guests: Their journey will be happy and comfortable, and they will arrive quickly.

Illness: Illnesses will be allayed.

Evil spirits: There are definitely no evil spirits bothering you. There is no cause for trouble even though the omens appear unpleasant, and so in actuality the situation is favorable. Pray to your special deity and this will clear your mind of the confusion.

Spiritual practice: If you practice the meditation of Vajra Saraswati then your intelligence will increase and this will be beneficial.

Lost article: If you employ skillful means, it will be found.

Will they come, and will the task be accomplished: You will accomplish it just as you wish.

All remaining matters: All of them are favorable. Perform peaceful activities; any activity involving women is especially good. For your own special deity, select any of the three Masters—Avalokiteshvara, Manjushri or Vajrapani—or any of the other Bodhisattvas. Also, it is good for you to rely upon the Mothers' Mandala of the Heruka family, the Clear Light practice, and the Yoga of Desire. You should recite such Tantras as the *Cakrasamvara* and *Vajra Dakini*, and sutras such as the *Samadhi Raja Sutra*. Perform ritual offerings to the Mamos, and rely upon Dharma Protectors such as the Damchen pair, the five Tsering Chedma goddesses, and peaceful protectors who appear riding an animal. Especially pray to Makzerma and Reti. In this way, whatever you wish or strive for with your mind, you will achieve.

This prediction is known as ''that which moves to pleasantly increase and expand one's intelligence.''

7. *RA AH, The Bright Lamp*

If RA AH—the bright lamp—appears, then one's own mind is very clear and excels, just as a lamp excels in dispelling darkness.

The sign of this divination is known as "the bright lamp without wind."

Family/property and life: These are currently favorable.

Intentions and aims: You can do just as you wish; there will be success.

Friends and wealth: The current situation is good.

Enemies: None will arise. You may hear that your enemies are a long way off, but they will not be able to harm you.

Guests: You will hear clear news about them, and their journey will be comfortable.

Illness: Your illness will get worse.

Evil spirits: There is no evil spirit bothering you. Your trouble is arising due to the power of previous deeds, but there will be no harm.

Spiritual practice: There will be no obstacles to your practicing by yourself.

Lost article: If you search in a southwesterly direction from where it was lost you will find it.

Will they come, and will the task be accomplished: If you commence with diligence there will not be any obstacles and it will be accomplished.

All remaining matters: No faults will be encountered in whatever activities you undertake. Read sutras such as the *Kalpa Bhadra Sutra*, and rely upon Lotus deities such as Amitayus, Kurukulli, Marici, and the like. If you practice the meditation of Humkara Father-Mother and Red Garuda then you will have success. Rely upon such Dharma Protectors as the great deity Tsimar. Obstacles will be prevented from arising by clearing roads and walkways, performing fire rituals, and so on, and in this way you will accomplish your wishes.

This prediction is known as "the one who helps oneself."

8. *RA RA, Adding Butter to the Burning Flames*

*If RA RA—the horse-headed deity Shri Hayagriva—
appears, then all activities of power will be accomplished
favorably and well.*

The sign of this divination is known as "to add butter again
and again to the burning flames of desire."

Family/property and life: These will increase well. Also, the
beauty of your body will be enhanced.

Intentions and aims: These will quickly be accomplished, and
you will also hear some clear news concerning them. If you
recite the proper number of mantras of any dakini practice,
then your activities will expand and be in sharper focus.

Friends and wealth: Any articles which are dry by nature and
of a red color will increase. Especially, by performing as many
power fire rituals as you can do then your happiness will increase greatly.

Enemies: Though there are no enemies opposing you, if you wish to attack, there will soon be clear news that you'll be able to destroy the enemy through the east or in the center.

Guests: They will arrive soon and their journey will be comfortable.

Illness: In order to cure such diseases as heat, blood and contagious illnesses, you need treatment as well as the performance of rituals. Other types of diseases will be quickly cured.

Evil spirits: There are no evil spirits attacking you. However, you are engaged in great works which are ill-planned, and so you are experiencing trouble. The attendants of the Wrathful Deities are not pleased with you, so if you make offerings to various types of worldly gods it will be good.

Spiritual practice: The performance of virtuous deeds and power activities will increase, and will be favorable for you.

Lost article: It will be found in a southern or western direction from where it was lost.

Will they come, and will the task be accomplished: They will be accomplished quickly.

All remaining matters: All are good, though any activities involving firm objects, earth and water are very bad. Engaging in them would be like water being exhausted through boiling or a summer pond being dried up. You should rely upon wrathful deities of the Lotus-family, and power deities such as Hayagriva and Takkiraja. Recite sutras and tantras of Avalokiteshvara, such as Amoghapasha. If you depend upon power and wrathful deities, then your purposes will be quickly achieved and you will be happy like a fire that flames up.

This prediction is known as "increasing the demonstration of joy."

9. *RA PA, The Demon of Death*

> *If RA PA—the demon of death—appears, then the symbol is destruction. Just as a spark of fire is extinguished by a small amount of water, so whatever work you engage in is non-virtuous and unsuccessful since it is clasped by the Lord of Death. The essence of this is that one departs through the outer southern door.*

The sign of this divination is known as "killing, death and destruction."

Family/property and life: There is death and great obstacles. To overcome these, clean scriptural texts of dust and dirt, and perform a torma-throwing ritual of some wrathful deity.

Intentions and aims: As there are great hindrances and obstacles, these will not be accomplished. It is best to postpone efforts to fulfill them.

Friends and wealth: There are no friends or wealth, and you will have obstacles in trying to gain them.

Enemies: There are enemies about. Especially, you must refrain from going in a southern or northern direction.

Guests: They will encounter an uncomfortable journey with obstacles on the path. Perform a White Umbrella Deity ritual.

Illness: There is a great danger to the ill person. Those with cold diseases or where water has accumulated in the body will have a very difficult time. If you don't recite mantras and perform rituals to the Protectors quickly and diligently, then it will be difficult to cure the disease.

Evil spirits: You are being harmed by impure drinking substances, round shaped articles which are dark blue in color, black articles such as certain types of food, wealth and ornaments of a widow, or pollutions arising from mixing your clothes together with the dirty clothes of a sick person or arising from the breaking of your vows. You should perform a releasing ritual (*ched drol*) of Tara or Vajrakilaya, and make offerings to the nagas. Even though the trouble comes from where you never suspect it, still you must protect yourself from unexpected troubles coming from water spirits, ghosts, and the like.

Spiritual practice: There are great obstacles. You should recite the Refuge Prayer to the Three Jewels one hundred thousand times. Also, perform the torma-throwing rituals and releasing rituals, and recite various sutras, and do other violent rituals directed towards the north. If these are not done, then it is very unfavorable. This divination shows great harm and obstacles to your life since it is like a flash fire which dies immediately. Recite the *Amitayus Sutra* and dharani as many times as possible.

Lost article: Though it has been taken in a southern or northern direction, you won't be able to see it again even if you trace it.

Will they come, and will the task be accomplished: Since there is a wrong intention involved, it will be obstructed and so cannot be accomplished.

All remaining matters: Though all inquiries will have a bad outcome, activities such as hunting, making poisons and acts of destruction will have favorable conclusions.

This prediction is known as "the activity which accomplishes destruction."

10.   *RA TSA, The King of Power*

If RA TSA—the king of power—appears, then spontane-
ous strength arises from oneself, just as a forest fire is in-
creased when stirred by the wind. Here, activities of power
and violence are endowed with sharp potential.

According to the essence of the words of the consort of Yamantaka, the Destroyer, the sign of this divination is known as "giving power to those who enter into this." This divination is also
known as "the roar of brave tigers and lions."

Family/property and life: As the strength of your power is
increasing, nothing whatsoever can harm you.

Intentions and aims: Being endowed with strength, whatever
you wish will be achieved. It is excellent to perform activities
of summoning and of violence. It is also good if you act in
accordance with the essential practice of your special meditation deity.

Friends and wealth: Your wealth will increase. Especially,
green articles and those of oblong or oval shape will increase.

Enemies: Since there are no enemies opposing you, you will be victorious over all classes of enemies.

Guests: Guests and visitors will have a comfortable journey and will arrive quickly. Also, you will meet with benefit.

Illness: Though your illness is acting up, there is no danger. You should make offerings to the Dharma Protectors.

Evil spirits: As the Protectors are guarding you, there are no evil spirits whatsoever troubling you. Though you think you have made great offerings to the Protectors, those are not enough and you must make even more offerings than before.

Spiritual practice: Whatever aims you have, they will be well achieved.

Lost article: It will be obtained through force.

Will they come, and will the task be accomplished: If you rely upon your special deity, they will come and all tasks will be accomplished.

All remaining matters: Though it is predicted that all remaining questions are favorable and your strength will be increased, know that any activity involving water, such as making rain, will have only mediocre results. Rely upon Vajrakilaya, the wrathful manifestation of Guru Padmasambhava, and your special meditation deity. By praising the power of the Dharma Protectors, you will be protected. If you offer incense and hang prayer flags, then all activities you wish to perform will be endowed with great power and so will be successful. If you rely upon the Dharma Protectors, Ganapati, Mahakala and the planet-demon Rahula, you will gain the spiritual attainments.

This prediction is known as "increasing power and strength."

11. RA NA, The Dried-up Tree

> *If RA NA—the tree that is not wet—appears, then know that there will be no result whatsoever, just as no fruit will come from a dried-up tree.*

The sign of this divination is proclaimed by the Gandharva (smell-eating being), the messenger of the demon Mara who resides in the southeast, who said, "Since one's mind is always afflicted, one's wishes are never achieved. So, this is suffering."

Family/property and life: Though there are no faults for the time being, in the future these matters will not go very well. Therefore, overall, the outlook is simply mediocre.

Intentions and aims: Being like a fire that suddenly flares up and then sputters out, they are difficult to accomplish.

Friends and wealth: There are none whatsoever.

Enemies: Although there are minor enemies, they are unable to cause you great harm.

Guests: Since the visitors will be tired and weary on their journey, there will be some delay in their arrival.

Illness: Although you will temporarily suffer from a bilious disorder, it will not be harmful to you.

Evil spirits: Through attachment to ancestors or relatives who have died, trouble is arising, but no harm will result. Through compassion, you should perform some rituals to repay your debt of kindness to deceased relatives. Further, as you have broken your wealth relationship with the local and earth gods, you should recite the *Suvarna Prabha Sutra* and various wealth propitiating rituals. It is good to accumulate merits, and also it is important to rectify disturbances caused by earth spirits whom you previously agitated.

Spiritual practice: Having too many wishes, it is hard for you to accomplish all of them—just as difficult as it is for a child to catch a rainbow.

Lost article: It has been stolen and hidden by another, so it will be difficult to recover.

Will they come, and will the task be accomplished: Since your wishes are influenced by others, your activities are like dreams. So, it will be difficult to see the results of achievement.

All remaining matters: These are not good. Especially, any inquiry regarding the wish to obtain happiness or a special article has a very unfavorable prognosis. Postponing a task will bring benefit. Rituals which could be performed to alleviate the problem are the recitation of the *Ten Wheels of Kshitigarbha*, and mantras or dharanis for increasing wealth and livelihood such as the *Suvarna Prabha Sutra*. Recitation of the *Manjushri Root Tantra* and the like is also good.

This prediction is known as "essenceless and inconceivable."

12. RA DHI,
The Door of Auspicious Visions

If RA DHI—the guard of the south—appears, then it is good, as this is the door of auspicious visions. Further, the eye of transcendental wisdom will open.

The sign of this divination is known as "summoning the goddess of the west as a friend."

Family/property and life: Your fortune will increase, and the quality of your life is good.

Intentions and aims: If you follow the advice of a good friend, then there will be success. Various practices for seeing visions upon mirrors and the like will also be successful.

Friends and wealth: If these are cultivated with diligence, then achievements will be made.

Enemies: There are none.

Guests: Their journey will be comfortable and they will arrive soon.

Illness: Rituals done for the sick person will enhance chances of an immediate recovery.

Evil spirits: There are none bothering you.

Spiritual practice: This is good. Especially, any practice which deals with the purification of precepts will be beneficial.

Lost article: If you search in a southern or western direction from where it was lost, it will be found.

Will they come, and will the task be accomplished: It will be accomplished.

All remaining matters: All are good, and you should quickly turn your mind from engaging in unsuitable, non-virtuous activities. It is advisable to rely upon Red Yamantaka. Further, your objectives and goals will increase and good signs will arise if you perform any religious practice involving voice goddesses, deities of the Lotus-family, goddesses such as Marici, and Dharma Protectors such as Dorje Lekpa. Read various sutras and tantras, and if you burn many butter lamps and recite the prayer to Guru Padmasambhava as many times as possible, then your intentions will be achieved.

This prediction is known as "advice from a beneficial friend."

13. *PA AH, The Vase of Nectar*

If PA AH—the vase of nectar—appears, then activities of peace are accomplished, just as a vase is filled with nectar.

The sign of this divination is known as "drink nectar and gain immortality."

Family/property and life: The outlook for these is good.

Intentions and aims: There are no obstructions whatsoever, so you will achieve your aims. There is great benefit in fulfilling the wishes of the guru just as he desires.

Friends and wealth: Just as you can obtain whatever you desire from a wish-fulfilling vase, so you receive benefit from friends and wealth.

Enemies: There are no enemies since all are endowed with a peaceful mind.

Guests: Visitors will arrive safely and quickly, but a child may have some obstacles or troubles on the journey and thus will not arrive as soon as expected.

Illness: Medical treatment and performance of rituals will become like nectar, benefiting you quickly.

Evil spirits: There are none bothering you whatsoever.

Spiritual practice: Performance of peaceful activities and the like is good. Further, it is favorable to rely upon deities that purify obscurations such as Vairocana (Sarva Vidya), the Medicine Buddha, Akshobhya and the like.

Lost article: Search in a southern direction, or near a pond or stream.

Will they come, and will the task be accomplished: Having accomplished the task, you will be glad and without regret though you won't be as satisfied by it as you had anticipated.

All remaining matters: All of these will turn out all right. However, any activities involving poison, and the like, will not be successful. All unfavorable conditions will be pacified if you perform washing rituals, rituals which lead beings to liberation at the time of death, confessions, and other purification rituals.

This prediction is known as "the turbulent activities involving relatives and peaceful people."

14. *PA RA, The Pool Without a Source of Water*

If PA RA—a pool without any source of water—appears, then wealth declines, just as a flow of water stops when its source is cut off.

The sign of this divination is known as "the assembly of demons residing in the southwest who are the messengers of Mara, said, 'What is the use of building a castle on the sandy shore of an ocean?' "

Family/property and life: Though there is no problem for the immediate future, in the long run the outlook is slightly unfavorable. Therefore, you should accumulate merit.

Intentions and aims: The outlook for the accomplishment of your aims is only mediocre, and no benefit can come from friends.

Friends and wealth: Though something will be obtained, it will neither last nor be of benefit.

Enemies: Although there are many enemies who are greater than you think, they will not be able to actually harm you.

Guests: The visitors will have regret for their journey, but they will not face failure. They will also have difficulty in arriving on time.

Illness: There will be physical disturbances of the body and great unhealthiness. You should perform as many repayment rituals and substitute rituals as possible.

Evil spirits: Although there is a little trouble arising from an article that was owned by a man and woman who separated and are resentful, still, since it cannot be identified, the harm will be minimal.

Spiritual practice: Good results will not be produced. You are undecided and confused. Furthermore, you have faulty and unwholesome intentions. Besides, the methods you are employing are not good. Therefore, you should recite confession prayers, the Prayer of Samantabhadra, the *Avatamsaka Sutra*, the *Kalpabhadra Sutra*, and other sutras. Also recite the *Lalita Vistara Sutra*; the reading of the *Prajnaparamita Sutra in Eight Thousand Verses* will be beneficial. Especially, recite the prayer and mantra of Guru Padmasambhava many times. The faithless must produce faith.

Lost article: Since that lost article is unusable, even if it is found it will be of no benefit to you.

Will they come, and will the task be accomplished: Though you will commence the task, it will be difficult to gain a good result.

All remaining matters: They are unfavorable. This is especially true for making relationships. Since destroying your goals is like destroying your work itself, it would be good to move to any other place, change your timings, and so on. Make many offerings of food and of other articles to the Sangha. Rely upon the dakinis such as Sang Ye and Simha Mukha. Also, it is good to perform burnt-food rituals, substitute rituals, and repayment rituals.

This prediction is known as "decreasing of happiness."

15. *PA PA, The Ocean of Nectar*

If PA PA—the ocean of nectar—appears, then wealth increases, just as the great ocean is filled with water.

The sign of this divination is known as "the saying of Ushnisha Vijaya, 'the summer river increases.' "

Family/property and life: They are currently good, and will increase.

Intentions and aims: You will obtain much wealth, prosperity and favorable conditions.

Friends and wealth: They will be inexhaustible like the water of a great ocean.

Enemies: No enemies will arise, and old ones will be reconciled.

Guests: Their journey will be comfortable and they will arrive on time.

Illness: If it is only a cold disease, then it is not bad. However, if it is a water disease, then the prospects of recovery are only fair.

Evil spirits: There are none whatsoever that are bothering you. However, there is a danger of increasing attachment due to meeting with others.

Spiritual practice: It is very good. Through the practice of peaceful activities, the spiritual attainment of peaceful activities will be achieved.

Lost article: It will be found either by a relative or by your searching in a northern or southern direction from where it was lost.

Will they come, and will the task be accomplished: All people involved are in harmony and so it will be accomplished effortlessly.

All remaining matters: The outlook for all is favorable and good, and food and drink will increase. Especially, any activity involving water is good. However, engagements, marriage and so on, and works involving fire are not so good. You should recite the *Avatamsaka Sutra* and various dharanis. Through cleaning images and making offerings to nagas, the obtainment of the objects of your wishes will increase. Also, if diseases and other disturbances are not very great, they can be allayed.

This prediction is known as "the washing that cleanses."

16. PA TSA, The Demon of Afflictions

If PA TSA—the demon of afflictions—appears, then happiness will be destroyed, just as the earth below the ocean is torn away by currents.

The sign of this divination is known as "the vicious Yaksha demon who dwells at the outer gate of the north said, 'The ocean was agitated and muddied by the tail of the malicious naga.' "

Family/property and life: There are obstructions and great disturbances.

Intentions and aims: For anything that you intend or aim, there are disturbance of mind and unhappiness.

Friends and wealth: The outlook is unfavorable; they are like dust being carried away by the wind.

Enemies: There is most probably an enemy. Especially, you will face harm from the east or north. There will most probably be a suit filed against you.

Guests: Those on the journey will be endangered by getting lost, having something broken, or falling.

Illness: There are air diseases and diseases of the veins and tendons that hamper movement. In order to remedy the pain you are experiencing from these, it is necessary to make torma offerings to the spirits and to perform the three parts ritual as many times as possible. Also, recite various sutras and the Prayer of Samantabhadra, release animals, and perform the Four Mandalas Ritual of Tara. It would be good to perform the meditation retreat of Acala as well.

Evil spirits: There is an attack of spirits belonging to the wood or green class. This is probably caused by a naga ritual or black magic being done against you. Also, you are being harmed by reciprocal fighting, people saying bad things against you, or by your having gone to gatherings where there is fighting and quarreling.

Spiritual practice: Your mind will be disturbed, agitated and unhappy. You will break your vows. Therefore, you should rely upon Acala, perform torma-repelling rituals of a wrathful deity, hang prayer flags, and clean the dust from Dharma books.

Lost article: The article went into the wrong hands and will not be recovered.

Will they come, and will the task be accomplished: Since your mind is very disturbed, it will be difficult to accomplish the task.

All remaining matters: They are unfavorable. Especially, the agitation of your mind and thoughts is great. However, there will be success in doing evil actions, such as causing people to separate, causing someone to leave you, and the like. There will be benefit by constructing small clay yellow stupas and other types of yellow stupas.

This prediction is known as "the boiling of agitation."

17. PA NA, *The Golden Lotus*

*If PA NA—the golden lotus—appears, then any aim what-
soever will be successful, just as green crops ripen into yellow kernels. Also, this is called "the unploughed harvest."*

The sign of this divination is known as "from the speech of
the very pleasing consort of White Manjushri who said, 'A
garden of mandara flowers moistened by the rain of nectar is
very beautiful.' "

Family/property and life: There are excellent conditions, so
these are very good.

Intentions and aims: They will become better and better.

Friends and wealth: These will increase and benefit you
greatly. Especially, if you perform wealth-propitiating rituals
of Vasudharani, Vaishravana, and Jambhala your wealth will
increase. You should also rely upon the Dharma Protector Men
Tsun.

Enemies: There are none against you.

Guests: Their journey will be comfortable and their purpose will be accomplished. However, the journey will be a little slow.

Illness: The disease will be cured gradually.

Evil spirits: There are none bothering you. Since many people look up to you, you can be of benefit to them.

Spiritual practice: Your good intentions will increase, and your teaching of the Dharma will gather people like bees and benefit them. It would be good to make an image of a Dharma Protector, and also to rely upon peaceful deities such as White Vajra Varahi and Vajra Devi. If you recite the *Lalita Vistara Sutra* and the *Bodhisattva Pitaka Sutra*, it will bring happiness and good luck in the future.

Lost article: It will be found. Even if it isn't found immediately, there is a good chance to find it in the future.

Will they come, and will the task be accomplished: It will be accomplished gradually.

All remaining matters: Though the outlook is not so positive for the present time, gradually it will become good.

This prediction that possesses beauty is known as "increasing happiness."

18. PA DHI,
The Nectar-like Medicine

If PA DHI—the doorman of the north—appears, then it is through the door of nectar-like medicine that benefit will arise. This is also called "the gathering of the clouds of the essence of gold."

The sign of this divination is known as "arriving at the happy stream in the golden south."

Family/property and life: All these matters are good.

Intentions and aims: Whatever you wish for will be accomplished just as you envision. Furthermore, you will be nourished by the fulfillment of your plans. If you rely upon deities such as Pratisara, your wishes will be achieved.

Friends and wealth: Your gains and wealth will increase greatly.

Enemies: There are none against you.

Guests: They will have a comfortable journey and will arrive on time.

Illness: If you act according to the doctor's advice the disease will be cured.

Evil spirits: There are none now, since the one that was bothering you has left.

Spiritual practice: Your character and behavior is pleasing, and so you will accomplish your practice in accordance with whatever you wish.

Lost article: If you search in a southern or northern direction from where it was lost, you will definitely find it.

Will they come, and will the task be accomplished: They will come, and the task will be accomplished.

All remaining matters: Just as the above answers have augured success, so likewise any other matter about which you may inquire will be successful. Assisting others to give up their bad intentions is good. If you practice peaceful activities through relying upon deities such as Akshobhya, White Sita Vajra Vidarana, and Amrita Kundali, then your good fortune and happiness will increase like the gems found in the ocean. Moreover, rely upon Guru Padmasambhava, deities of the Jewel-family, wealth deities, and deities of the increasing-class. Also, it will be beneficial to rely upon peaceful Dharma Protectors. Make praises and offerings to White Mahakala and hang blue prayer flags. If you place the *Prajnaparamita Sutra* in water, and the like, then your relatives will say beneficial and nice things to you, and you will be well received when you arrive at a place.

This prediction is therefore known as "similar goodness."

19. *TSA AH, The White Umbrella of Good Fortune*

If TSA AH—the great umbrella of good fortune—appears, then good fortune increases, just as the white umbrella flutters.

The sign of this divination is known as "the flower garden that ripens on time."

Family/property and life: These matters are in good condition.

Intentions and aims: They will be fulfilled. Performing the meditation and recitation of Simha Mukha is beneficial. Especially, you will hear good news. However, your decisions will sometimes have no effect and others' promises will not have any results, like the imprint of a bird's feet in the sky.

Friends and wealth: If you make offerings to the wealth deities, good news will most probably come.

Enemies: There are none, so you do not need to be apprehensive.

Guests: They will have a comfortable journey and will arrive soon.

Illness: You will recover quickly.

Evil spirits: You are bothered, not by evil spirits, but rather only by your mental imputations. There is no reason for your troubles other than the propensities of your own conceptualizations.

Spiritual practice: This will be successful.

Lost article: There is an average chance of finding it.

Will they come, and will the task be accomplished: There is an obstruction, so the undertaking will not occur whatsoever.

All remaining matters: The prediction is called "giving breath." Therefore, you should rely upon deities such as Dhvaja Devi, Tashi Lhamo, and Maha Mayuri. It is also good for you to hang prayer flags and construct prayer wheels. If you pray to protectors like Pehar it is good.

This prediction is known as "whatever path one desires to travel upon, one will arrive safely."

20.   TSA RA,
The Great Fiery Weapon

*If TSA RA—the great fiery weapon—appears, then one
is successful, just as one receives a reward for bravery, having been victorious over all.*

The sign of this divination is known from the words of Yamantaka, the chief of the wrathful army who destroys the enemy,
the destroyer of those with wrong understanding, who roared,
"Defeat the enemy, subdue Mara."

Family/property and life: Diligently and continually perform
rituals to the protectors. Then things will be very good.

Intentions and aims: Being victorious over every direction leads
to success. Especially, there is great success for the Dharma
activity of wrathfulness, such as subduing others, and the like.
Just by the recitation of wrathful mantras, and so on, there
will be success.

Friends and wealth: Wealth, food, drink and the like will be
obtained through force.

Enemies: All enemies will be destroyed, and you will be victorious over others.

Guests: They will come quickly and will be victorious over others.

Illness: Illness will be cured.

Evil spirits: They don't have the chance to look at you, let alone to trouble you. You are so strong that you have the ability to keep the mind of others under your control, so you should produce compassion for them.

Spiritual practice: Power and violent activities will produce clear results.

Lost article: It will be found.

Will they come, and will the task be accomplished: It is certain to be accomplished.

All remaining questions: This prediction deals with the act of showing strength in all matters. Generally, the performance of works involving earth and water will encounter difficulty. Such activities as causing thunderbolts, hail, and the like will be accomplished. Rely upon the meditation deities with wrathful mantras, and Yamantaka. If you rely upon the meditations and practices involving fire and air, such as the path of inner heat and the melting of the Bodhicitta to produce bliss, then you will have an excellent ability to accomplish power and violent activities. You should rely upon Yamantaka, Hayagriva, Mahakala, and male deities of the Activity-family such as Amoghasiddhi. By relying upon Vajrakilaya you will gain power. It is specially good to rely upon Maning, Mahakala, Leshin or Vajrapani.

This prediction is known as "subduing all others by being endowed."

21. TSA PA, Empty of Intelligence

*If TSA PA—empty of intelligence—appears, then thoughts
are empty, just as the wind moves through an empty valley.*

The sign of this divination is known from the town-dwelling
evil spirits and ghosts, the messengers of Mara that wander
in the northwest, who said, "It is very difficult to catch a white
piece of paper carried away by the wind; who is capable of
catching it?"

Family/property and life: Though they meet with unfavorable conditions and there is great danger of their being separated, scattered and destroyed, still the performance of rituals
will be of benefit.

Intentions and aims: You are becoming too worried and men-
tally aggravated for such a small purpose.

Friends and wealth: Even if wealth is held in your hand, it
will seep through like water leaking from cupped hands.

Enemies: Though the nature of this enemy was first friendly
and then later hateful, still there wouldn't be any greater harm

than to have a disputation with him. It is best to stay away from him and give some money that will benefit him.

Guests: They will turn back empty-handed or will have difficulty in fulfilling their desired purpose.

Illness: There will be a slight cold or air disease, and your body's elements are out of balance. The reason for the increase in your mental afflictions is due to the power of your relationship with bad friends and bad attendants. Separating from them will bring happiness. Your activities will most probably be polluted.

Evil spirits: Though there is no great harm from them, still you should perform a substitute ritual.

Spiritual practice: As your mind is very agitated, it will be difficult to accomplish your wishes.

Lost article: It will be difficult to recover.

Will they come, and will the task be accomplished: As this is the divination "empty of intelligence," it is difficult to accomplish.

All remaining matters: It is predicted that they won't be achieved as you wish. Most probably, people will not listen to your advice. Make your mind steady, accumulate merit, read the Vinaya, and recite collections of sutras.

This prediction is known as "scattering the mind into pieces".

22.   TSA TSA, The Streamer of Fame

If TSA TSA—the streamer of fame—appears, then one's renown and fame will increase, just as the king of the gods resounds the drum when victorious in war. This is the divination of Garuda's son flying in the sky.

The sign of this divination is known from the words of Amrita Kundali who said, "This is the time for proclamations in every direction, just as one hoists a flag at the summit of a mountain."

Family/property and life: Generally speaking, the current situation of your family/property and life is positive, and your good fortune will increase. Nonetheless, when excessiveness surpasses excessiveness, you will need to catch in small pieces only (i.e., only small things will be accomplished).

Intentions and aims: There will be success in fulfilling your wishes. If you diligently perform rituals to the Dharma Protectors, then any activity you have begun will be accomplished.

Friends and wealth: Most probably you will obtain them quickly.

Enemies: Though there will be fighting, you will be victorious.

Guests: The journey will be comfortable and they will return quickly. Also, you will hear news of them.

Illness: Although the body is out of balance due to an air disease, there is no danger or cause for concern.

Evil spirits: There are none that are bothering you.

Spiritual practice: There will be great success in fulfilling your aims. Also, you will obtain great renown.

Lost article: You will most probably find it quickly by searching in a northeasterly direction from where it was lost.

Will they come, and will the task be accomplished: It is predicted that they will come.

All remaining matters: They are successful and stable. However, you will face difficulties with activities involving earth and water. You should rely upon making offerings, reciting praises and performing rituals against curses. Rely upon the meditation practice of wrathful Niladanda, the goddess Tsanti, and also upon the Dharma Protectors such as Cittapati and Ngen Nema, as well as activity deities. Such activities as traveling, flying in the sky, walking with fast feet, and so on, will meet with success. Success will also be experienced in any activity of expelling, such as expelling ghosts from a certain locale. It is good to make various types of offerings, such as tea, scarves, and the like.

This prediction is known as "quick settlement and fame."

23.   *TSA NA,*
The Mara Demon of Aggregates

*If TSA NA—the Mara of the aggregates—appears, then
matters pertaining to family, property, life, friends, and
wealth are not positive whatsoever, just as a tree is cut
down in the middle.*

The sign of this divination is known from the words of the
"slaughterer of breath" who resides at the outer eastern gate
who said, "Cut plants with a sickle."

You must recite mantras for a long time and perform torma-
throwing rituals.

Family/property and life: The outlook is unfavorable.

Intentions and aims: There is a great obstruction. The "air
horse" (i.e., good luck) won't run on the path. Recite the prayer
of Guru Padmasambhava, *Removing Obstacles from the Path,*
and also the *Sutra of Tara Which Dispels the Darkness in the
Ten Directions.*

Friends and wealth: The outlook for both having beneficial
friends and gathering wealth is not good.

Enemies: Most probably you will encounter an enemy. Especially if you remain in the eastern or central part of your country, you will be suppressed. Perform a ritual for subduing enemies, such as that of Ta Mar or King Kang. Since you may be scolded and berated by your superiors, you should think ahead in order to prevent this from happening.

Guests: There will be obstacles on the journey. It will be difficult for them to arrive on schedule, and they will have remorse for having undertaken the journey.

Illness: There is a strong phlegm disease, and there will be difficulty in breathing. Rituals are needed to overcome this.

Evil spirits: You are being harmed by earth spirits and local spirits. Also, you are experiencing trouble caused by a yellow article, and a square house, square room, or any square object . You may also be harmed by a "king evil spirit" who is following an article given to you from the house or from the hand of a Buddhist or Bon priest. The cause of this is your desire to compete with the people who originally inhabited that place or with great non-humans, or your harming of images, and the like. There is also a great danger of being afflicted by impurities and pollutions, so the washing ritual should be performed.

Spiritual practice: Though you think about the Dharma path, you are diverted to wrong directions. In order to overcome this, you should clean roads, build paths nicely, and rely upon obstacle-clearing deities such as Tara.

Lost article: As the meat has already entered the mouth of the lion, it is difficult to recover.

Will they come, and will the task be accomplished: Although there is much commotion, it won't be accomplished.

All remaining matters: They are not favorable. However, acts of instigation or deception will meet with success.

This prediction is known as "being pressed down by a large hill."

24. *TSA DHI,*
The House of Good Tidings

> *If TSA DHI—the gatekeeper of the east—appears, then good works are accomplished, just as the house of good tidings is seen. Also, this is called the wish-fulfilling tree.*

The sign of this divination is known as "to adorn your work with the streamers of transcendental activity."

Family/property and life: All of these matters will have good and sudden results. The work of informing others is especially good.

Intentions and aims: These will be successful, with quick results. Relations with others are good.

Friends and wealth: There will be success with immediate results. Relaying news is especially good.

Enemies: There are none, and you will experience a pleasant time.

Guests: They will have a comfortable journey, meet with good friends and will arrive soon.

Illness: Your disease will be cured.

Evil spirits: There are none that are bothering you.

Spiritual practice: Good intentions are involved and so your spiritual activities will increase.

Lost article: It will be found in an eastern or northern direction from where it was lost.

Will they come, and will the task be accomplished: It will be successfully completed, and you will be able to settle matters.

All remaining matters: In accordance with your desires, you will find success. Rely upon Activity-family deities such as Mahabala, Parna Shavari, Ushnisha Vijaya, and Tara. Make offerings to the four-armed Mahakala and other Dharma Protectors. It is also good to rely upon Ma Gyal and Yaksha-family deities. Recite sutras from the Ratna Kuta Collection. It is good to study and teach the Dharma. There will be benefit in having conch shells blown and making adornments of streamers.

This prediction is known as "dissemation of joyful news and arrival at the summit of the mountain."

25. *NA AH, The Golden Mountain*

If NA AH—the golden mountain—appears, then firm-
ness and stability are seen, just as the golden mountain
reaching high is seen.

The sign of this divination is known as "the unchanging auspicious symbol."

Family/property and life: These matters are firm and steady.

Intentions and aims: These are excellent and will bring stability to your life in the future.

Friends and wealth: The possessions and friends obtained earlier are stable, and they will remain due to the power of steadiness.

Enemies: There are none whatsoever, and your power is steady.

Guests: Though they are neither lost nor harmed, they will take a little time to arrive.

Illness: There is none.

Evil spirits: There are none whatsoever bothering you.

Spiritual practice: It is firm and good through strength and steadiness.

Lost article: It has not gone into another's hands.

Will they come, and will the task be accomplished: Though there may be a delay of your present project in favor of another, that project which has already been started will meet with a successful outcome.

All remaining matters: Generally, all of these are successful. However, any activity involving travelling to another place will encounter some delay. Read the *Avatamsaka Sutra* and Vinaya Sutras. Rely upon deities of the Vajra-family and mother deities of the Destroyer-family. Hold Kshitigarbha as your special deity. Your good fortune will increase if you rely upon the mantras of Locani, Vaishravana and Jambhala. Erect images and stupas and perform activites which are steady.

Since this prediction is known as "holding one's own place and not moving," it represents the excellence of all activities performed on a stable foundation.

26. NA RA,
The Demon of the Heavenly Son

*If NA RA—the Mara demon of the heavenly son—
appears, then this fall of the dice augurs ill, just as a fire
burns a good house.*

The sign of this divination is known from the words of the
deceiver, the great leader of wrong views, who dwells at the
outer gate in the west, who said, "If the fire of desire blazes,
oneself is burnt."

Family/property and life: There is instability and great obstruction.

Intentions and aims: The result of completion is empty.

Friends and wealth: They are similar to the ashes of burnt
silk and silken brocades.

Enemies: There are enemies, and harm will especially arise
from the southwest.

Guests: There is a great danger for both man and property.

Illness: You are suffering from a disease such as a hot disease, blood disease, or contagious disease, and it is bad.

Evil spirits: A red article, a triangular article, or flesh and blood from the west is causing you harm. There is danger of being harmed by spirits if you burn things in the kitchen or displease them in other ways.

Spiritual practice: To avert a great obstacle, perform peaceful fire rituals and washing rituals many times. Make medicines and recite various prayers and mantras of Guru Padmasambhava many times.

Lost article: It will not be found.

Will they come, and will the task be accomplished: There is a danger of not accomplishing the task, since there is a great obstacle.

All remaining matters: They are not successful. However, the prospects are excellent for non-virtuous activities such as setting fire to a city. It is good to do "cutting rituals," and the like.

This prediction is known as "the aggregates of the person being harmed by suffering."

27. *NA PA, The Overflowing Jewelled Vessel*

If NA PA—the golden vessel filled with grains—appears, then prosperity increases, just as the jewelled vessel is filled with food. This is also called the wish-fulfilling cow.

The sign of this divination is known from the words of White Manjushri, whose body causes deterioration to be allayed who said, "The concurrence of the golden vase and the ingredient of nectar is very beautiful."

Family/property and life: They are in positive state and are endowed with happiness.

Intentions and aims: The happiness of mind increases.

Friends and wealth: Food, wealth and friends, in particular, return and increase.

Enemies: There are no thieves and enemies.

Guests: Their purpose will be successful. Though a litttle late, they will arrive happily.

Illness: It will be cured and you will gain happiness.

Evil spirits: There are none that are bothering you. Though it appears like an attack from an evil spirit, it is actually a favorable condition.

Spiritual practice: It is good and will meet with success.

Lost article: Either it will be found in the eastern part or central area of your locale, or it will be found in a southern direction from where it was lost.

Will they come, and will the task be accomplished: If they have not yet come to your place or not yet begun the work, there will be some regret but the endeavor will be accomplished in the future just as they had wished.

All remaining matters: You should remain happy and contented. Receive empowerments and initiations, and rely upon wealth deities and deities of the Jewel-family. If you practice the yoga technique of extracting the essence of food and the process of creation, you will meet with success. Perform consecrated food offerings and rituals to the Dharma Protectors, and make offerings to the nagas. Recite the Vairocana Tantra. Also, relying upon Ganapati is good.

This prediction is known as "the good field which increases happiness."

28. NA TSA, The Scattered Mountain of Sand

If NA TSA—the mountain of sand—appears, then the results of your aims are spoiled and thrown about, just as dust is scattered by the wind.

The sign of this divination is known from the speech of the mind-stealing spirits, the messengers of the demon Mara who dwell in the northeast, who said, "The golden house is gradually levelled into dust."

Family/property and life: They will be diminished more and more.

Intentions and aims: There will be great changes, and finally you will experience deterioration.

Friends and wealth: Nothing new will arise, and your previously accumulated possessions will greatly diminish.

Enemies: Since your prosperity will suddenly be harmed by enemies, you must perform suppressing rituals.

Guests: You will be happy to see them, but the news they bring will cause repentance and sorrow.

Illness: It doesn't appear to be an illness that causes great harm; this slight illness can be cured through religious rituals.

Evil spirits: Though there is not a great evil spirit, still your mental perceptions have been agitated and disturbed. You should perform a peaceful fire ritual. The cause of this disturbance is that you have accumulated propensities for faulty activities and decisions. A burying ritual should be performed. Request members of the Sangha to recite verses of auspiciousness.

Spiritual practice: Since the future is not good, it will be difficult to achieve your goals.

Lost article: It will be more difficult to find it as time passes.

Will they come, and will the task be accomplished: It will be difficult to accomplish. Even if it is accomplished, there will be no benefit derived from it.

All remaining matters: There will be no meaningful result of your activities. However, works involving destruction will be successful. As this prediction is unfavorable, you should recite the *Ratna Kuta Sutra*, the *Mangala Sutra*, and prayers to Guru Padmasambhava many times, and build a golden bridge. It is also beneficial to perform a burying ritual and have scriptures written with gold lettering.

This prediction is known as "dwindling the mountain into dust."

29. *NA NA, The Mansion of Gold*

> *If NA NA—the mansion of gold—appears, then all things are good, vast, and stable, just as a celestial mansion is endowed with vast wealth.*

The sign of this divination is known as "where the jewelled mountain is set upon a ground of gold there is great astonishment."

Family/property and life: Since the present conditions are like an inexhaustible treasure, these matters are seen to be excellent through great steadfastness.

Intentions and aims: Just as the earth and mountains are very firm, so these are good. However, there is a chance of delay. If you propitiate wealth deities and earth deities, your aims will be achieved.

Friends and wealth: These resources will be very vast in the future.

Enemies: They do not exist for you.

Guests: Their arrival will be delayed, but since they arrive safely, their trip is well accomplished.

Illness: Though you will suffer for a long time from a serious illness, no lasting harm will arise from it. Furthermore, it is difficult for another illness to arise.

Evil spirits: There is no cause for any evil spirit to harm you.

Spiritual practice: You will be steadfast in keeping vows and the like, and your wishes will be fulfilled.

Lost article: It has not moved from the place where it was lost. If, by chance, it has been moved, then it will be difficult to recover.

Will they come, and will the task be accomplished: Unless the matter is settled quickly, there is a chance of delay.

All remaining matters: If they are not delayed, they will turn out well. It will be difficult to accomplish unsteady activities such as giving up your job, moving, going to new places, making requests to officials, and the like. Also, activities involving destruction are not favorable. Activities involving wealth rituals, binding, hastily done works, and so on, are excellent. Erect shrines for wealth deities, such as Vasudharani, and also erect stupas. Bury a wealth vase in your house. To practice increasing activities is very good. Recite the mantras of Buddha Locani and Kshitigarbha. Rituals performed for Ber Nag Chen Mahakala are also beneficial.

This prediction is known as "the placing of some great thing upon another great thing."

30. NA DHI, The Treasury of Jewels

If NA DHI—the gatekeeper of the west—appears, then there is perfect prosperity, similar to the opening of a treasury of jewels.

The sign of this divination is known as "opening the door of the treasury of jewels in the east". It is also known as "obtaining butter from milk and gems from the ocean."

Family/property and life: As there will be no changes, prospects are good.

Intentions and aims: They are excellent and firm, and so the outlook for the future is positive.

Friends and wealth: Whatever you wish will be fulfilled.

Enemies: None will arise.

Guests: They will have a successful and comfortable journey.

Illness: It will gradually clear up.

Evil spirits: There are none whatsoever bothering you.

Spiritual practice: It is very good. It is recommended that you rely upon deities of the Vajra-family and the three masters of the Tathagata-family. Also, rely upon Mahabala.

Lost article: It must be near to the place where it was originally lost.

Will they come, and will the task be accomplished: In the long run, it will be accomplished.

All remaining matters: They are successful. It is especially advisable to seek the blessings of the Jewel-family. If you rely upon nagas and other spirits, there will be success. Make offerings to earth deities and local deities so that good luck will arise. This prediction is known as "a building of many stories."

31. *DHI AH, Manjushri Appears*

If DHI AH—the brave Manjushri—appears, then whatever is wished for will be fulfilled, like a gem falling into one's hand.

The sign of this divination is known from the speech of the Transcendental Being of Mind's Great Bliss who said, "The agility of the great primordial wisdom of pure awareness increases without regard to directions."

Family/property and life: Since they are firm and without obstructions, they are good condition.

Intentions and aims: Have no doubts concerning the situation, since an authority that is not involved with deception is present here. It is advisable to listen to, study and contemplate the general Buddhist teachings, especially those of the mantra teachings.

Friends and wealth: They will continue to increase.

Enemies: All enemies will come to you with respect.

Guests: Their journey will be comfortable and successful.

Illness: It will be cured naturally.

Evil spirits: There are none whatsoever that are disturbing you now, nor will any arise. The situation is good, and there is no cause whatsoever to be harmed, so do not worry.

Spiritual practice: It is good, and the happiness of your mind will increase. Whatever you wish will be fulfilled.

Lost article: It will be found.

Will they come, and will the task be accomplished: They will come and it will be accomplished.

All remaining matters: All your goals will be fulfilled. Rely upon meditation deities such as Manjushri, Padmasambhava, Kalacakra, and the like. Meditate upon the path of the Illusory Body and the Six Applications of the Great Completion. Also rely upon Thang Lha and Mahakala as your Dharma Protectors. If you erect the three supports of images, scriptures and stupas, then most probably you will encounter prosperity.

This prediction is known as the "principal owner of the thirty-six cities" or "increasing transcendental wisdom and accomplishing excellence."

32. *DHI RA,*
The Endless, Auspicious Knot

If DHI RA—the auspicious knot—appears, then a mind-pleasing scene will be witnessed, just as when one arrives at a flower garden.

The sign of this divination is known as "oh, intelligent one, look at that wonderful scene with your eyes."

Family/property and life: The outlook is not merely good, but is excellent.

Intentions and aims: Your intentions are appropriate and will meet with success. In relation to people, your dwelling, and events happening at your present residence, good fortune will occur. Whatever your decisions may be, only harmony will arise. For this reason, plans and aims will meet with success and happiness and be well accomplished.

Friends and wealth: You will gain both, along with joy.

Enemies: There are none.

Guests: Their journey is comfortable and they will arrive soon.

Illness: It will be cured soon.

Evil spirits: There do not appear to be any bothering you. There is no cause for any to trouble you, so your mind should be at ease and happy.

Spiritual practice: Your wishes will be fulfilled and advancements will begin to appear.

Lost article: It will be found quickly.

Will they come, and will the task be accomplished: It will be accomplished and they will come.

All remaining matters: It is best for you to do what you think is right. Rely upon auspicious deities such as Nivarana Vikshambhi, Ushnisha Vijaya, Sita Tapatra, and the like. If you rely upon Cakrasamvara, Vajrasattva and Mahajala it is especially good, and you will fulfill your wishes. Reciting the prayer of Spontaneously Fulfilling Wishes of Guru Padmasambhava is certain to bring success. Simply practicing the meditation deities which you previously relied upon, and propitiating the Dharma Protectors that you cherished in your heart, will bring good fortune.

This prediction is known as "friendly desire."

33. DHI PA, The Golden Female Fish

If DHI PA—the golden female fish—appears, then physical agility and good luck will increase, like the swift movements of a female fish in the ocean.

The sign of this divination is known as "because one bathes in nectar, one's happiness increases."

Family/property and life: Their prospects are good.

Intentions and aims: These are favorable and successful.

Friends and wealth: They will arise in great number.

Enemies: They have no chance to harm you.

Guests: Their journey will be comfortable and they will arrive quickly.

Illness: It will be cured.

Evil spirits: There are none to bother you.

Spiritual practice: It is good and progress will be made.

Lost article: It will be recovered.

Will they come, and will the task be accomplished: They will come to fruition in time.

All remaining matters: They will be smooth, good, and will succeed. Studying medicine is positive. Recite the *Ratna Kuta Sutra*, the *Smrityupasthana Sutra*, and other short sutras. If you do peaceful and increasing fire rituals, you will meet with good results. Also, holding Maitreya as your special deity is good.

This prediction is known as "to endeavor in accordance with one's intentions, wishes and aims."

34. DHI TSA, The White Conch

If DHI TSA—the white conch of Dharma—appears, then fame and fortune increase, like the pleasant sound of the conch.

The sign of this divination is known as "one's thoughts become renowned like a pleasing tune."

Family/property and life: The outloook is positive, and you will hear good news.

Intentions and aims: These will be successful, and you will hear good tidings. If you teach languages, debate, logic and the like, it is good.

Friends and wealth: You will hear some very clear news.

Enemies: There are none.

Guests: They will arrive with good news.

Illness: Though there is no danger or harm to the ill person's life, agitation and disturbance of the mind will occur.

Evil spirits: There are none to bother you.

Spiritual practice: Fame will come to you.

Lost article: There will be clear news about it.

Will they come, and will the task be accomplished: They will come, and it will be accomplished.

All remaining matters: They will succeed, so do as you wish. You should hold Arya Samantabhadra as your special deity. Recite the *Dhvajagra Sutra* and various dharanis. Rely upon Caturmukha and Yaksha-family deities for Dharma Protectors. As others will agree with you, you will accomplish your desires.

This prediction is known as "increasing good news and fame."

35. *DHI NA, The Golden Wheel*

If DHI NA—the golden wheel—appears, then there is prosperity and well-being, like the obtaining of a kingdom by a prince. There is prosperity and well-being.

The sign of this divination is known as "the amazement of obtaining a treasure without effort."

Family/property and life: They are stable and good.

Intentions and aims: Because they are steady in the long run, the prospects are good. Especially, you will be foremost in worldly customs and manners.

Friends and wealth: They will increase.

Enemies: They will come under your control.

Guests: They will be victorious and happy.

Illness: Though there is definitely no danger to the sick person, since some god is displeased with this person, he or she will take a little while to recover.

Evil spirits: There are none bothering you.

Spiritual practice: There will be good luck and it will succeed.

Lost article: There is a possibility of finding it at another time.

Will they come, and will the task be accomplished: There will be some delay, but the future is good.

All remaining matters: In the long run there will be success. Rely upon meditation deities such as Yamantaka, the unsurpassable Heruka, Vairocana, and the like. Also, rely upon Ushnisha Cakravartin as your special deity. Recite the Mara Vijaya Dharani. Also, it is advisable to rely upon Panjara Mahakala and Caturmukha as your Dharma Protectors.

This prediction is known as "climbing upon a throne."

36. *DHI DHI,*
The Jewelled Banner of Victory

*If DHI DHI—the hoisted banner of victory—appears,
then you are victorious and excel, like the raising of the
banner of victors over every direction. You are able to accomplish whatever activity you wish to do.*

The sign of this divination is known as, "If one relies upon
the powerful wish-fulfilling king, then greater and greater
results are obtained. This is truly amazing."

Family/property and life: Since your family and property do
not diminish, it is good. As your life force is very stable, it
is hard like a diamond, so there is no present worry about sick-
ness or death.

Intentions and aims: These will be very well fulfilled. It is
good to make nectar pills and perform the meditation practice of deities who hold swords and other similar objects.

Friends and wealth: They will be gathered. Your desires are
fulfilled by the wish-fulfilling jewel so that your aims and wishes
are accomplished in a way exceeding your expectations.

Enemies: There are none.

Guests: They will have a comfortable journey and will arrive safely.

Illness: It will be cured naturally.

Evil spirits: There is neither an evil spirit troubling you nor a cause for one to trouble you.

Spiritual practice: It is clear and bright like the moon outshining the stars. If you diligently meditate upon your special deity, you will gain great attainments. If you study logic, you will be particularly successful.

Lost article: If you do as a close friend advises you, then it will be found.

Will they come, and will the task be accomplished: All your tasks work out smoothly, and there will be success.

All remaining matters: All these matters will meet with success, so you should do as you wish to do. Through accumulating more virtues and relying upon meditation deities such as Vajrakilaya, Hevajra, Guhyasamaja, Vajrapani, and the like, you will meet with much good luck and good fortune. If you make offerings to the six-armed Mahakala it is good. You should recite the texts of the Great Completion and the *Manjushri Nama Samgiti*. Also, rely upon the Dharma Protector King Gesar as Werma.

This prediction is known as "hoisting the jewelled banner of victory."

Glossary

Acala: (Tib. *Mi yo wa*) The enlightened deity known as the Immovable One who assists one to overcome obstacles.

Activity of increasing: (Tib. *Gyas pa'i las*) The tantric practice that deals with augmenting one's own or others' qualities. It involves exercises that lengthen life, and increase prosperity, merit, and the like.

Activity of peace or purification: (Tib. *Zhi wa'i las*) The tantric practice that deals with the disposal of obstacles through peaceful means such as recitation of mantras of purifying deities (for example, Vajrasattva), confession of one's non-virtuous actions, and the like.

Activity of power or subduing: (Tib. *Wang wa'i las*) The tantric practice that deals with the effort to bring various forces under one's own control.

Activity of violence, destruction or wrathfulness: (Tib. *Drak pa'i las*) The tantric practice that deals with the overcoming of major obstacles through seemingly violent methods in order to bring about a peaceful environment. Concerning violent activities and wrathful deities, see Rene De Nebesky-Wojkowi's *Oracles and Demons of Tibet* (Graz, Austria:

Akademische Druk-u. Verlagsantstalt, 1975).

Akashagarbha: (Tib. *Nam kha'i nying po*) One of the eight great Bodhisattvas, who assists supplicants to purify broken vows of the Mahayana tradition.

Akshobhya: (Tib. *Mi truk pa* or *Mi kyob pa*) The Buddha of the eastern direction who is blue and who is master of the Vajra-family.

Amitabha: (Tib. *Od pak med*) The Buddha of the western direction who is red and who is master of the Lotus-family. See *Sukhavativyuha*, Buddhist Mahayana Texts, Part II, trans. F. Max Mueller (New York: Dover 1969).

Amitayus: (Tib. *Tse pak med*) The Buddha of longevity. Through performing meditation upon him, one is able to gain a longer lifespan.

Amitayus Sutra: (Tib. *Tse do*) The discourse which explains the qualities of the Buddha Amitayus and the practices related to him.

Amoghapasha: (Tib. *Don yod shak pa*) A manifestation of the Bodhisattva Avalokiteshvara who assists in the purification of any downfalls in moral conduct.

Amoghasiddhi: (Tib. *Don yod drup pa*) The Buddha of the northern direction who is green and master of the Activity-Quality-family.

Amrita Kundali: (Tib. *Dud tsi kyil ba*) A wrathful-appearing tantric deity who especially helps to purify the location in which rituals or practices are to be performed.

Avalokiteshvara: (Tib. *Chen ray zi*) The enlightened being who embodies the compassionate nature of all the Buddhas.

Avatamsaka Sutra: (Tib. *Pal cher do*) One of the largest of all Mahayana discourses, it describes interrelatedness and non-obstruction of the various enlightened and unenlightened states as seen from the Buddha's viewpoint. See Thomas Cleary's

English translation, *Flower Ornanment Scripture* (Boston: Shambhala, 1985).

Ber Nag Chen Mahakala: (Tib. *Gon po ber nag chen*) A manifestation of the great protector of the Dharma especially propitiated by the Karma Kargyud tradition.

Bodhicitta: (Tib. *Chang chub kyi sem*) The great altruistic resolve and determination to gain the state of full and perfect enlightenment for the sake of all sentient beings. Also, a term used in the Vajrayana that refers to semen.

Bodhisattva: (Tib. *Chang chub sem pa*) A being who is cultivating the path to full enlightenment for the sake of bringing all sentient beings to that state of ultimate freedom and peace.

Bodhisattva Pitaka Sutra: (Tib. *Chang chub sem pa'i de nod*) A discourse of the Buddha dealing with the vows and practices of the Bodhisattva.

Bon or Bonpo: The indigenous religion of Tibet found before the advent of Buddhism there. See David Snellgrove's *Nine Ways of Bon* (Boulder: Prajna Press, 1980).

Book of the Perfection of Wisdom: (Tib. *Yum gyal* or *Phar chin do*; Sanskrit *Prajnaparamita Sutra*) Any one of a number of Mahayana scriptures dealing with the Buddha's teaching on ultimate truth or wisdom.

Book of the Perfection of Wisdom in Eight Thousand Verses: (Tib. *Gyed tong pa*; Skt. *Ashtasahasrika Prajnaparamita*) See Edward Conze's English translation (London: Four Seasons Foundation, 1973).

Buddha: (Tib. *Sang gye*) A fully and perfectly enlightened being whose wisdom, compassion and skillful means endow him to work for the happiness and enlightenment of all sentient beings.

Buddha Avatamsaka Sutra: See Avatamsaka Sutra.

Burnt food ritual: (Tib. *Sur ngo*) A ritual in which certain types of food are placed upon an open fire in order to make offerings especially to those beings who can receive nourishment only through smell (such as those passing through the intermediate state between death and rebirth).

Burying ritual: (Tib. *Si nen*) This is a violent and complicated ritual in which certain objects are buried in order to overcome major obstacles.

Butter lamps: (Tib. *Cho me*) A very popular practice among Tibetan Buddhists is to burn votive lamps or candles in temples or at personal shrines. Butter was the principal oil used for this purpose in Tibet, and for that reason they became known as butter lamps.

Cakrasamvara: (Tib. *Dem chog*) A tantric deity of the highest class of the Tantras.

Caturmukha: (Tib. *Zhal zhi pa*) The four-faced Mahakala, a Dharma Protector especially worshipped by the Sakya and Gelugpa traditions.

Circumambulation: (Tib. *Khor wa*) A religious practice used for the purpose of accumulating merit, in which a person walks around a sacred object such as a temple or shrine, always keeping it to his right.

Cittipati: (Tib. *Dur throd dak po*) The protectors of the Cakrasamvara Tantra who take the form of a pair of skeletons.

Clear light practice: (Tib. *Od sal*) A tantric practice which involves the methods to realize the clear light, or ultimate nature, of mind. See *Esoteric Teachings of the Tibetan Tantra*, ed. C.A. Muses (York Beach, Maine: Samuel Weiser, 1982) and W.Y. Evans-Wentz's *Tibetan Yoga and Secret Doctrines* (Oxford: Oxford University Press, 1969).

Confession prayers: (Tib. *Shak pa*) The prayers or discourses which involve the method for demonstrating regret for the past performance of non-virtuous deeds. See *Mahayana Purifica-*

tion (Dharamsala: Library of Tibetan Works and Archives, 1980).

Cutting Ritual: (Tib. *Chod*) This is a ritual and meditation to forcefully cut attachment to one's own ego-clinging or self-grasping.

Dakini: (Tib. *Kha dro*) A class of female deities who are the manifestation of the feminine energies of enlightenment.

Damchen pair: Two Dharma Protectors worshipped especially in the Nyingma school.

Deity: (Tib. *Yidam* or *lhak pa'i lha*) Generally speaking, this refers to a Buddha or Bodhisattva (or a manifestation of one of them) that one employs for the purpose of devotional exercises or visualization in a tantric practice. See Walter Eugene Clark's *Two Lamaistic Pantheons* (New York: Paragon Book Reprint Corp., 1965), B. Bhattacharyya's *Indian Buddhist Iconography* (Calcutta: Mukhopadhyaya, 1958), and A. Getty's *Gods of Northern Buddhism* (Rutland: Tuttle Press, 1977).

Dharani: (Tib. *Zung*) A form of mantra.

Dharma: (Tib. *Cho*) The teaching of the Buddha.

Dharma Protectors: (Tib. *Cho sung, cho kyong* or *sung wa*) A class of enlightened beings who manifest in a wrathful appearance for the sake of protecting the teachings.

Dhvajagra Sutra: (Tib. *Gyal tsen tse mo do*) A discourse concerning the victory of the gods over the demi-gods.

Dispelling the Darkness in the Ten Directions: (Tib. *Chok chu mun sel*) This is a discourse concerning the savioress Tara.

Dorje Lekpa: A Dharma Protector propitiated especially by followers of the Nyingma tradition.

Earth deities or spirits: (Tib. *Sa dak*) A class of sentient beings who claim ownership of the locale in which they reside.

Expelling ritual: (Tib. *Dud dok*) A violent tantric ritual in which evil forces are expelled from the locale in which they are causing harm.

Extracting the essence of food: (Tib. *Chud*) A practice in which one extracts the essential nature of some object for the purpose of gaining nourishment, longevity, health, and the like. It includes drawing the essence out of flowers, stones, nectar pills, and meditation, as well as other objects.

Families: (Tib. *Rig*) According to the Vajrayana teaching, it is said that the various Buddhas, Bodhisattvas and other enlightened beings can be classified in five major families, known as Buddha Races. These five families are known as the Vajra, Tathagata, Jewel, Lotus and Activity or Quality families.

Father-Mother: (Tib. *Yab yum*) A form that tantric deities assume in which they appear as male and female in sexual union.

Fire ritual: (Tib. *Jin sek*) A complicated tantric ritual in which a deity is invoked in the midst of a fire and numerous prescribed articles are offered.

Four Mandalas Ritual of Tara: (Tib. *Drol ma man dal zhi cho ga*) A ritualistic offering made to the savioress Tara for the purpose of gaining merit and overcoming different types of obstacles. During this ritual, the universe in the form of a mandala (or symbolic representation of the world) is offered four times.

Ganapati: (Tib. *Tshok dak*) The elephant-faced deity who is especially propitiated by followers of the Sakya tradition.

Gandharva: (Tib. *Dri za*) These sentient beings, who are said to exist through extracting their nourishment from odors, are well known for their accomplishment as celestial musicians.

Garuda: (Tib. *Khyung da*) The powerful, horned bird of Indian culture is considered also a tantric deity and worshipped especially by followers of the Sakya tradition.

Green Tara: (Tib. *Drol ma jang gu*) This "savioress" or female Bodhisattva is the embodiment of active compassion. Though appearing in many forms and colors, the green form is most worshipped and is extremely popular among Tibetan Buddhists. See Stephan Beyer's *Cult of Tara* (Berkeley: University of California Press, 1973), and *In Praise of Tara, Songs of the Saviouress*, Martin Willson, trans. and ed., (London: Wisdom Publications, 1986).

Guhyasamaja: (Tib. *Sang ba du pa*) A tantric deity of the highest class of Tantra, and also the name of a tantric discourse. See Alex Wayman's *Yoga of the Guhyasamaja Tantra* (Delhi: Motilal Banarsidass, 1977).

Guru Padmasambhava: See Padmasambhava

Guru-yoga practice: (Tib. *Lama'i naljor*) The tantric practice of meditation upon one's guru in order to cultivate faith and to gain his blessings.

Hayagriva: (Tib. *Tam din*) A red deity who is the wrathful manifestation of Avalokiteshvara.

Heruka: A tantric deity especially employed in the Nyingma tradition.

Hevajra: (Tib. *Kye dorje*) A tantric deity of the highest class, primarily practiced in the Sakya tradition. Also a discourse known as the Hevajra Tantra. See David Snellgrove's *Hevajra Tantra* (Oxford: Oxford University Press, 1959).

Humkara: (Tib. *Hum dzed*) A tantric dcity used for warding off hindrances.

Illness/disease: According to Tibetan medicine, diseases are classified into several main categories, such as hot disease, cold disease, air disease, and phlegm disease. These diseases are related to different internal organs which have become afflicted, or to various imbalances within the body's or mind's structure. There are several book available that give good information about Tibetan medicine, such as Bhagwan Dash's *Tibetan Medicine* (Dharamsala: Library of Tibetan Works and

Archives, 1976), Yeshe Donden's *Health Through Balance* (Ithaca: Snow Lion Publications, 1986) and Ven. Rechung Rinpoche's *Tibetan Medicine* (Berkeley: University of California Press, 1976).

Illusory Body: (Tib. *Gyu ma'i lu*) A tantric practice in which one seeks to realize the illusory or untrue nature of one's body and the world. See Garma C.C. Chang's *Six Yogas of Naropa and Teachings on Mahamudra* (Ithaca: Snow Lion Publications, 1986) and W.Y. Evans-Wentz's *Tibetan Yoga and Secret Doctrines* (Oxford: Oxford University Press, 1969).

Inner heat: (Tib. *Tummo*) A tantric practice in which a strong heat or fire is caused to awaken within one's body for the purpose of purifying the inner, subtle veins and elements so that higher tantric practices can be accomplished.

Interdependent Origination: (Tib. *Ten drel*, Skt. *pratityasamutpada*) In a literal sense, this is the Buddha's teaching of the twelve links or causal conditions that explain the cause and continuation of a person's birth and rebirth in the world of existence. From the relative point of view, it represents the conditional existence of all phenomena, while, from an ultimate point of view, it expresses the emptiness or inherently selfless nature of all phenomena.

Jambhala: (Tib. *Zam bha la*) A tantric deity of wealth.

Kalacakra: (Tib. *Du khor*) Literally meaning "The Wheel of Time," this is the name both of one of the tantras and of the main deity found in that teaching. See the Dalai Lama and Jeffrey Hopkin's *Kalacakra Tantra* (London: Wisdom Publications, 1985).

Kalpa Bhadra Sutra: (Tib. *Do de kal zang*) A discourse of the Buddha in which the thousand Buddhas of the present aeon are named and described.

King Evil Spirit: (Tib. *Gyal po'i don*) A class of evil spirits known for their mischievous and violent nature.

King Gesar: The great folk king of Tibet known for his exploits in conquering evil in the world. See Alexandra David Neel's *Superhuman Life of Gesar of Ling* (Boston: Shambhala Publications, 1987).

Kshitigarbha: (Tib. *Sa yi nying po*) One of the eight great Bodhisattvas. See *Sutra of the Past Vows of Earth Store Bodhisattva* (San Francisco: Buddhist Text Translation Society, 1980).

Kurukulli: (Tib. *Rig ched ma*) A female deity renowned for her activity of controlling various forces and energies.

Lalita Vistara Sutra: (Tib. *Gya cher rol pa'i do*) A discourse describing the life of the Buddha.

Lama: A spiritual teacher.

Leshin: A wrathful deity found in the form of a protector.

Locani or Buddha Locani: (Tib. *Sang gye chen ma*) A manifestation of a female enlightened being and the spiritual consort of Vairocana.

Long-life meditations/rituals: (Tib. *Tse drup*) These are practices designed for overcoming the possibility of untimely death as well as to increasing one's life span. Generally, they are related to deities of long life, such as Amitayus, White Tara and Ushnisha Vijaya.

Mahabala: (Tib. *Thob chen*) A Bodhisattva possessing great power who assists those encountering various types of hindrances.

Mahakala: (Tib. *Gon po* or *Nag po chen po*) "The Great Black One" is a wrathful manifestation of a protector utilized to overcome obstacles that one may encounter. Can appear with four or six arms.

Maha Mayuri: (Tib. *Ma cha chen mo*) A tantric deity.

Mahayana: (Tib. *Theg pa chen po*) The "Great Vehicle" of the Buddhist tradition which emphasizes the attainment of full and perfect enlightenment for the sake of all sentient beings.

Maitreya: (Tib. *Cham pa gon po*) One of the eight great Bodhisattvas, he is recognized to be the next Buddha.

Makzerma: A female protector sometimes also known as Mahakali.

Mamo: A class of female spirits generally evil in nature though sometimes employed as protectors of the teaching.

Mandala: (Tib. *Khyil khor*) The abode or residence of a deity. These are symbolically shown in the form of geometric diagrams and used for the meditative purpose of entering into the realm or state of the deity. See Giuseppe Tucci's *Theory and Practice of the Mandala* (New York: Samuel Weiser, 1978).

Mandara flowers: A very rare type of flower said to appear only on very auspicious occasions, such as the time of the Buddha's birth.

Mangala Sutra: (Tib. *Tashi tseg pa do*) A discourse of the Buddha recited at auspicious times in order to bring happiness for the occasion.

Mani: Here it is used as the abbreviated name of the mantra of Avalokiteshvara, Om Mani Padme Hum.

Mani prayer wheel: A cylindrical case filled with mantras, in this case Mani mantras, that is turned in a clockwise direction for the purpose of gaining merit.

Manjushri: (Tib. *Jam pal yang*) The Bodhisattva or enlightened being who manifests the wisdom of all the enlightened Buddhas and Bodhisattvas.

Manjushri Nama Samgiti: (Tib. *Jam pal tsen jod*) A discourse which centers around the Bodhisattva Manjushri. See Alex Wayman's *Chanting the Names of Manjushri* (Boston: Shambhala Publications, 1985).

Manjushri Root Tantra: (Tib. *Jam pal tsa gyud*) A discourse of the Vajrayana tradition.

Mantra: (Tib. *Ngak*) A group of letters or syllables, usually originating from the Sanskrit alphabet, that may literally or symbolically express the qualities of a deity. These syllables may also assist a person to bring his or her own mind under control or to bring some other forces under control.

Mara: (Tib. *Dud*) Those internal and external factors or forces which obstruct one's spiritual path. There are four Maras which are known as the demonic forces of the afflictions, aggregates, death and the heavenly son (likened to a demonic cupid).

Mara Vijaya Dharani: (Tib. *Dud tsar chod pa'i zung*) A mantra recited to help one overcome Mara.

Marici: (Tib. *Od zer chen ma*) A female deity worshipped in order to overcome various types of fear.

Mayajala: (Tib. *Gyu trul da wa*) A tantric deity.

Medicine Buddha: (Tib. *Sang gye men la*) The enlightened being whose primary vow is to aid those afflicted with illness. See Raoul Birnbaum's *Healing Buddha* (Boulder/Boston: Shambhala Publications, 1979), Ven.Rechung Rinpoche's *Tibetan Medicine* (Berkeley: University of California Press, 1976) and Bhagwan Dash's *Tibetan Medicine* (Dharamsala: Library of Tibetan Works and Archives, 1976).

Melting of the Bodhicitta: A higher tantric practice involving the controlled movement of semen within the body.

Men Tsun: A being considered to be an ancestral spirit.

Mo: Divination or any system of making predictions.

Naga: (Tib. *Lu*) A class of beings related to water and sometimes known as snake spirits. Generally, diseases related to the skin are said to be caused by them.

Nectar pills: (Tib. *Dud tsi ril bu*) These are pills, predominently composed of herbs, made by the Lamas. Though used for religious rituals and practices, they are eaten by the lay community chiefly as a blessing coming from the Lama for the purpose of overcoming disease and to act as a purifying agent.

Niladanda: (Tib. *Yug ngon chen*) A Bodhisattva worshipped for his great power.

Nivarana Vikshambhi: (Tib. *Drip pa nam sel*) One of the eight great Bodhisattvas.

Non-humans: (Tib. *Mi ma yin*) A class of mischievous spirits who appear as humans but actually are not.

Nyingmapa: The "Old Tradition," the original school of the Vajrayana to arise in Tibet.

Padma Sambhava: (Tib. *Pema jungnay*) The great Indian master who established the Vajrayana teaching in Tibet, popularly known in Tibet as Guru Rinpoche. See Yeshe Tsogyal's *Life and Liberation of Padmasambhava* (Berkeley: Dharma Publishing, 1978).

Panjara Mahakala: (Tib. *Gur gi gon po*) The "stick-wielding great black one" who is the protector of the Hevajra teaching and those who practice that teaching. He is the special protector for the Sakya tradition.

Parna Shavari: (Tib. *Lo kyon ma*) A female deity worshipped for her ability to assist those afflicted by diseases, especially contagious diseases.

Peaceful activities: See Activity of peace.

Pehar: A special protector worshipped by the Nyingma Tradition.

Pollutions: (Tib. *Drib*) Defilements acquired through coming into contact with impure objects, such as a corpses or dirty clothes of an ill person, or through contaminating oneself with impure actions such as breaking on one's vows, incestuous relations, quarrels, and the like. The belief is that such pollutions can cause different kinds of physical and mental disturbances.

Prajnaparamita Sutra: (Tib. *She rab kyi pha rol tu chin pa'i do*)
The Mahayana scriptures dealing with the Buddha's teaching
on the Perfection of Wisdom. See translations of some of these
by Edward Conze, *Selected Sayings from the Perfection of Wisdom* (Boulder: Prajna Press, 1978), *Large Sutra of Perfect Wisdom* (Berkeley: University of California Press, 1975), *Buddhist
Wisdom Books: The Diamond Sutra and the Heart Sutra* (London: George Allen and Unwin, 1970), and *Short Prajnaparamita
Texts* (London: Luzac, 1973).

Pratisara: (Tib. *So sor drang ma*) A deity worshipped by those
seeking to have children.

Prayer flags: (Tib. *Lung ta*) Cloth hangings on which mantras
and prayers of various deities or elemental forces are printed
for the purpose of gaining good fortune and luck. Sometimes
these are also called "wind horses," since they are thought
to produce a windfall or good luck.

Prayer of Samantabhadra: (Tib. *Sang chod mon lam*) This is
the prayer of the great Bodhisattva Samantabhadra that is
recited in all Tibetan monasteries and considered to possess
great blessings. See Kalsang Gyaltsen's *Aspirations of
Samanatabhadra* (Silver Springs: Sakya Center).

Prayer wheel: A cylindrical case filled with mantras that is
turned in a clockwise direction for the purpose of gaining merit.

Process of completion: (Tib. *Dzog rim*) The second of the two
stages of the Vajrayana path leading to liberation and enlightenment. This stage primarily involves meditations dealing with
control of inner body functions, such as breath, movement
of subtle fluids within the body, and the like.

Process of creation: (Tib. *Kyed rim*) The first of the two stages
of the Vajrayana path leading to liberation and enlightenment.
This stage primarily involves practice dealing with visualiza-
tions, recitation of mantras, and the like.

Prostrations: (Tib. *Chak tsal wa*) A popular Tibetan practice in which one prostrates in front of a shrine for the purpose of generating faith, purifying one's non-virtues and gaining merit.

Rahula; planet-demon Rahula: (Tib. *Da dzin*) A protector of the Nyingma Tradition.

Ratna Kuta Sutra Collection: (Tib. *Kon chok tsek pa'i do*) A collection of short Mahayana discourses. See Garma C. C. Chang's *A Treasury of Mahayana Sutras* (University Park, Pennsylvania: Pennsylvania University Press, 1983).

Ratnasambhava: (Tib. *Rin chen jung den*) The Buddha of the southern direction who is yellow and master of the Jewel-family.

Red Yamantaka: (Tib. *Shed mar*) A tantric deity of the highest class of Tantras.

Refuge prayer: (Tib. *Kyab dro*) The prayer that Buddhists recite to reaffirm their faith in the Three Jewels.

Releasing ritual: (Tib. *Ched drol*) A ritual in which negative forces are released from the hold they possess over someone.

Removing Obstacles from the Path: (Tib. *Bar ched lam sel*) A prayer written by Guru Padmasambhava.

Repayment rituals: (Tib. *Jal che*) A ritual of making offerings to enlightened beings and to ordinary sentient beings for the purpose of repaying any karmic debt one may have accrued from them, whether in this lifetime or in some past lifetime.

Reti: (*Remati*) A female protector of the Nyingma tradition.

Rituals to the Dharma Protectors: (Tib. *Kangso*) A liturgy involving ritualistic offerings to the protectors of the teaching.

Rituals which lead beings to liberation at the time of death: (Tib. *Phowa*) The practice of "phowa" in which oneself or a qualified practitioner guides the dying person through the stages of death so that he or she will be able to gain a state of liberation at that very time. See Khenpo Konchog Gyaltsen's *In Search of the Stainless Ambrosia* (Ithaca: Snow Lion Publications, 1988), Garma C.C. Chang's *Six Yogas of Naropa and Teachings on Mahamudra* (Ithaca: Snow Lion Publications, 1986) and W.Y. Evans-Wentz's *Tibetan Yoga and Secret Doctrines* (Oxford: Oxford University Press, 1969).

Samadhi Raja Sutra: (Tib. *Ting nge dzin gyal po'i do*) A major Mahayana discourse discussing various meditative states.

Samantabhadra: (Tib. *Kun tu zang po*) One of the of the eight great Bodhisattvas.

Sangha: (Tib. *Gendun*) Those who follow the teachings of the Buddha, especially those who have taken the vows of a renunciate.

Saraswati: (Tib. *Yang chen ma*) The goddess of learning and of the arts.

Scarves: (Tib. *Kha ta*) White strips of fringed silk which are ceremonially used for making offerings to a shrine or a Lama, when meeting someone, or at farewells.

Shakyamuni: (Tib. *Shakya thub pa*) The Buddha, also known as the "sage of the Shakya clan," thus Shakyamuni.

Simha Mukha: (Tib. *Seng dong ma*) The lion-faced wrathful female deity worshipped in order to overcome obstacles, such as black magic directed at oneself.

Sita Tapatra: See White Umbrella deity.

Smrityupasthana Sutra: (Tib. *Dran nyer zhak pa'i do*) A Mahayana discourse.

Special deity: (Tib. *Yidam*) The deity with whom one has a special relationship, helping one's accomplishment of the tantric path.

Spontaneously Fulfilling Wishes: (Tib. *Sam lhun*) A prayer written by Guru Padmasambhava.

Stupa: (Tib. *Chod ten*) A reliquary holding the remains of an enlightened being or marking the spot where a great spiritual deed was accomplished. See Lama Anagarika Govinda's *Psycho-cosmic Symbolism of the Buddhist Stupa* (Berkeley: Dharma Publishing, 1976).

Subduing Enemies Ritual: (Tib. *Gyal do*) A ritualistic enactment of subduing those who are creating harm to others.

Substitute ritual: (Tib. *Lud tor*) A ritual in which an article that represents an afflicted person is ritualistically offered to those evil forces causing the harm. The article is offered as a substitute for the actual person, so that the harm directed towards that person is now redirected towards the article instead. In this way, the afflicted person's troubles are averted.

Suppressing ritual: (Tib. *Da nen*) A violent tantric ritual in which evil is suppressed in a complicated ritualistic manner.

Sutra: (Tib. *Do*) A discourse of the Buddha.

Suvarna Prabha Sutra: (Tib. *Ser od do*) A Mahayana discourse.

Takkiraja: (Tib. *Dod pa'i gyal po*) A tantric deity often found in conjunction with Kurukulli and Ganapati. Within the Sakya tradition these three deities are known as the Three Red Ones.

Tantra: (Tib. *Gyud*) A discourse of the Buddha that deals with the Vajrayana.

Tara: (Tib. *Drolma*) See Green Tara.

Tashi Lhamo: The goddess of good luck.

Thang Lha: A protector seen riding on a horse.

Three Jewels: (Tib. *Kon chok sum*) This term refers to the Buddha, his teaching which is known as the Dharma, and his followers who are collectively known as the Sangha. These three are the very basis or foundation of the entire Buddhist faith.

Three parts ritual: (Tib. *Cha sum cho ga*) A ritual of the lower class of Tantras used for purifying a locale and averting problems.

Three Roots: (Tib. *Tsa sum*) This term refers to the Guru or teacher, a person's special or personal meditation deity (known as a Yidam), and Dakinis who are a class of female deities who are the manifestation of the feminine energies of enlightenment.

Three times: (Tib. *Du sum*) The past, present and future.

Torma: A special food offering, usually made of barley powder, that is specifically designed for different deities.

Torma offerings: (Tib. *Tor ngo*) A ritual in which the tormas are offered to various deities, especially to the Dharma Protectors.

Torma-throwing ritual: (Tib. *Tor dok*) A violent tantric ritual in which the torma is conceptualized as a weapon and thrown in the direction of those evil forces creating troubles.

Tsimar: A protector of the teaching who was stationed at Samye Monastery (the first Buddhist temple ever built in Tibet) by Guru Padmasambhava.

Ushnisha Cakravartin: (Tib. *Tsuk tor khor lo gyur wa*) One of the ten wrathful Bodhisattvas specified in the Vajrayana for assisting in overcoming obstacles.

Ushnisha Vijaya: (Tib. *Tsuk tor nam gyal ma*) A white female deity worshipped in order to receive the blessings of longevity.

Vairocana: (Tib. *Nam par nang dzed*) The Buddha of the central realm who is white and master of the Buddha or Tathagata-family.

Vaishravana: (Tib. *Nam say*) The guardian deity of the northern direction of the world who is also known as the king of wealth deities.

Vajra: (Tib. *Dorje*) The indestructible or infallible diamond nature which is able to destroy everything but is not harmed or flawed in return. The supreme symbol of the Vajrayana path, the vajra is shown in the form of a five- or nine-pronged scepter and is used ritualistically by the practitioner. Though containing many symbolic meanings, it is said to represent primarily the powerful skillful means needed to gain the various stages leading to full enlightenment.

Vajra Dakini Tantra: (Tib. *Dorje kha dro ma'i gyud*) A Vajrayana discourse.

Vajradhara: (Tib. *Dorje chang*) The manifestation of the highest Buddha or aspect of full and perfect enlightenment found in the Vajrayana tradition.

Vajrakilaya: (Tib. *Dorje Phurba*) A tantric deity of the highest class of Tantras who is seen holding a mystic dagger, and who is especially worshipped by the Nyingma and Sakya schools, the teaching concerning this deity was spread by Guru Padmasambhava.

Vajrapani: (Tib. *Chak na dorje*) The enlightened being who holds a vajra in his hand and is considered to be the embodiment of the spiritual power of all the Buddhas and Bodhisttvas.

Vajra posture: (Tib. *Dorje kyil trung*) The meditation posture in which both legs are fully crossed, with the soles of the feet facing upwards.

Vajrasattva: (Tib. *Dorje sempa*) Though this tantric deity is known as a form of the highest aspect of enlightenment, he is especially meditated upon for the purpose of purifying the meditator's non-virtues, sins and downfalls.

Vajrayana: (Tib. *Dorje theg pa*) This is the Buddhist path of the tantric tradition. The discourses which were taught by the Buddha or one of his manifestations that included the esoteric teachings centering around visualization of deities, recitation of mantras or physical practices such as yoga and breathing exercises became collectively known as the Vajrayana or Buddhist Tantras. See S.B. Dasgupta's *An Introduction to Tantric Buddhism* (Boulder: Prajna Press, 1971).

Vasudharani: (Tib. *Nor gyu ma*) A female wealth deity.

Verses of auspiciousness: (Tib. *Tashi monlam*) Prayers and benedictions recited for bringing happiness and auspicious omens.

Vinaya: (Tib. *Dulwa*) The discourses of the Buddha dealing with the rules of moral conduct for the ordained followers. See these in the Sacred Books of the East Series, vols. 13, 17, and 20 (Delhi: Motilal Banarsidass, 1975) and Charles S. Prebish's *Buddhist Monastic Discipline* (University Park, Pennsylvania: Pennsylvania State University Press, 1975).

Violent rituals: See Activities of violence.

Walking with fast feet: (Tib. *Kang gyuk*) A practice by which a person is able to walk at incredibly fast speeds. For a story of this, see Alexandra David-Neel's *Magic and Mystery in Tibet* (New York: Dover, 1971).

Washing ritual: (Tib. *Tru*) A ritualistic ablution or cleansing of sins and other misfortunes through bathing with consecrated water.

Wealth deities: (Tib. *Nor lha*) A class of tantric deities who are propitiated in order to gain wealth.

Wealth-propitiating rituals: (Tib. *Yang drup*) Rituals directed toward specific wealth deities for the purpose of gaining wealth.

Wealth vase: (Tib. *Bum ter*) A vase filled with prescribed articles, which is consecrated and buried beneath a person's house in order to bring good fortune and prosperity to that residence and those living there.

White Mahakala: (Tib. *Gon kar*) A manifestation of the four-armed Mahakala, who appears white and is worshipped as a wealth deity.

White Manjushri: (Tib. *Jam yang kar po*) The white manifestation of the Bodhisattva of wisdom, Manjushri.

White Sita Vajra Vidarana: (Tib. *Nam jom kar po*) A tantric deity of the highest class of Tantras.

White Tara: (Tib. *Drol kar*) A manifestation of the savioress Tara who is white and is meditated upon for the purpose of gaining longevity.

White Umbrella deity: (Tib. *Duk kar*) A white female deity who holds an umbrella and is known for her power to alleviate wars, charms and other misfortunes.

White Vajra Varahi: (Tib. *Dorje phakmo karmo*) A female tantric deity meditated upon for gaining long life.

Wish-fulfilling cow: A cow that possesses an inexhaustible supply of milk and who can fulfill all of one's wishes.

Wish-fulfilling jewel: A splendid gem that grants each and all of one's desires.

Wish-fulfilling king: The king of all wish-fulfilling jewels.

Wish-fulfilling tree: A celestial tree that bears fruits of whatever type one wants.

Wrathful deities: (Tib. *Drak pa'i lha*) A class of tantric deities who take a wrathful or ferocious appearance in order to symbolize the method for the practitioner to overcome his own hatred as well as to overcome great hindrances to the accomplishment of his spiritual path.

Yaksha demon: (Tib. *Nod jin*) A class of spirits, often seen to be evil.

Yamantaka: (Tib. *Shin je shed*) A tantric deity of the highest class of Tantras who is the wrathful manifestation of Manjushri and is especially practiced by the Sakya and Gelug schools.

Yoga of desire: (Tib. *Dod pa'i naljor*) A tantric practice in which a consort is taken in order to accomplish higher levels of realization. See H.V. Guenther's *Life and Teaching of Naropa* (Boston: Shambhala Publications, 1986).